TIME

The Middle East

The History • The Cultures • The Conflicts • The Faiths

THE MIDDLE EAST

Editor Kelly Knauer
Design Ellen Fanning
Picture Editor Patricia Cadley
Writer/Research Director Matthew McCann Fenton
Copy Editor Bruce Christopher Carr
Maps Joe Lertola, Lon Tweeten

Time Inc. Home Entertainment

Publisher Richard Fraiman
Executive Director, Marketing Services Carol Pittard
Director, Retail & Special Sales Tom Mifsud
Marketing Director, Branded Businesses Swati Rao
Director, New Product Development Peter Harper
Financial Director Steven Sandonato
Assistant General Counsel Dasha Smith Dwin
Book Production Manager Jonathan Polsky
Marketing Manager Joy Butts
Design & Prepress Manager Anne-Michelle Gallero

Special thanks to: Bozena Bannett, Alexandra Bliss, Glenn Buonocore,
Barbara Dudley Davis, Suzanne Janso, Robert Marasco, Brooke McGuire,
Chavaughn Raines, Mary Sarro-Waite, Ilene Schreider, Adriana Tierno,
Cornelis Verwaal

Cover photography credits

Front cover, main image: Dome of the Rock: Richard T. Nowitz—Corbis

Top insets, left to right: Poppy Harvest, Kandahar: Victor R. Caivano—
AP/Wide World; Hamas headband: Ahmed Jadallah—Reuters—Landov;
Rafik Hariri murder: Mahamed Azakir—Reuters—Landov; Afghan girl: Brennan
Linsley—AP/Wide World

Bottom insets (no order): Crucifix carving: Natan Dvir—Polaris; Israeli flag:
Ziv Koren—Polaris; Koran: Majid—Getty Images

Back cover: Har Homa Israeli settlement, West Bank: Q. Sakamaki/Redux

SCOTT PETERSON—GETTY IMAGES

The Middle East

The History • The Cultures • The Conflicts • The Faiths

TIME

Contents

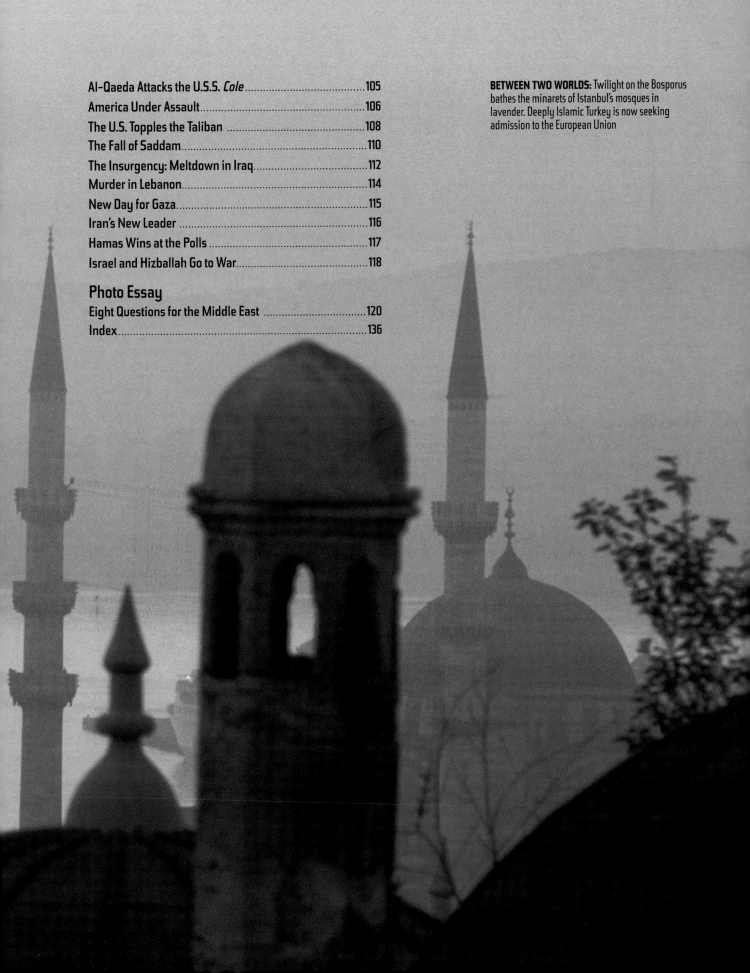

BETWEEN TWO WORLDS: Twilight on the Bosporus bathes the minarets of Istanbul's mosques in lavender. Deeply Islamic Turkey is now seeking admission to the European Union

Introduction by Jimmy Carter

VOICES OF WAR: An Israeli policeman and a Palestinian civilian square off in Jerusalem at the contested sacred site, the Dome of the Rock, in 2000

WHEN I WAS HONORED WITH THE NOBEL PEACE PRIZE in 2002, my thoughts settled on the memory of two friends, Egypt's President Anwar Sadat and Israel's Prime Minister Yitzhak Rabin, who were also Nobel laureates and who gave their lives for the cause of peace in the Middle East. Their sacrifices, and those of many others, brought this dream closer to reality—but a lasting peace still remains elusive.

Why? Every indication is that substantial majorities on both sides of the Israeli-Palestinian divide support the outlines of a compromise agreed to at Camp David in 1978 and in Oslo in 1993. Those agreements were based on the only reasonable prescription for peace: United Nations Resolution 242, which condemns the acquisition of territory by force, calls for the withdrawal of Israel from occupied territories and provides for Israelis to live securely and in harmony with their neighbors.

Yet in the decades since 1967, when the Security Council enacted Resolution 242, various leaders on both sides of the issue have vowed never to accept these fundamental terms. While such strident boasting can easily be mistaken for bravery, it is the antithesis of courage.

Courage is what defined men like Sadat and Israel's Prime Minister Menachem Begin, who took great risks simply by agreeing to negotiate with each other and risked even more by coming to an agreement. Courage was what drove Rabin to turn away from armed force and negotiate with Palestine Liberation Organization chief Yasser Arafat. Courage is what propels Palestinian President Mahmoud Abbas to continue his principled embrace of the terms of the Oslo Accords and the international "road map," while extremists within both Israel and the Palestinian territories do everything in their power to make them irrelevant. In short, courage—the vital commodity that is always in short supply—is what we most need more of.

Many people argue today that the Middle East peace process is dead. I disagree but do believe that it has been dangerously, tragically dormant. We see the evidence of this everywhere: the destructive conflict between Israel and Lebanon; the construction of an intrusive barrier wall in the

VISIONS OF PEACE: Anwar Sadat, Carter and Menachem Begin celebrate their successful Camp David summit, 1978

West Bank to extract more Jewish territory from Palestinian areas; and the rising prominence of extremists on all sides.

One of the first steps in reviving the peace process must be more American engagement. That too will require courage. The United States must push both sides to overcome the obstacles that stand in the way of peace. Into the existing vacuum have flowed unilateral moves by Israel and the growing strength of militants on the Palestinian side. History has proved that even when they are ready to negotiate directly, both Israelis and Palestinians need an objective and credible third party to help guide them through the process. In the past, America has been the only power that is acceptable to both sides and able to lead the international community in implementing any agreement.

The resumption of such American leadership is crucial, because the stakes have never been higher, in the Holy Land and across the region. The world community must not permit Iran to develop a nuclear arsenal, but threats of military attack and telling the Iranians that no discussion will begin until they have agreed, in advance, to American de-mands hardly gives them an incentive to negotiate. Refusing to conduct a dialogue with Syria gives that nation an incentive to tap its considerable potential for sowing discontent.

But the ultimate key to peace in the Middle East is the question of Israel and Palestine. For more than a half-century, following the founding of the state of Israel in 1948, the Middle East conflict has been a source of worldwide tension. In my new book, *Palestine Peace Not Apartheid*, I review this history and offer new ideas about how to build a better future. Although the book is sure to be controversial, I believe it is also a realistic and reasonable appraisal of how we may break the current deadlock and move forward. Doing so, by whatever means, would remove one of the major causes of international terrorism and greatly ease tensions that still have the potential to spark a regional or even global conflict. ∎

Jimmy Carter is the 39th President of the U.S.; the founder of the nonprofit Carter Center, which seeks to advance peace and health worldwide; and the winner of the 2002 Nobel Peace Prize. His many books include, most recently, Palestine Peace Not Apartheid

Birthplace of Three Religions

The desert environment and soaring sky of the Middle East reduce life to its essentials. Yet that very simplicity seems to nourish the life of the spirit, for here three of humanity's great faiths were born. Judaism, Christianity and Islam all trace their ancestry to the Old Testament figure Abraham, and followers of each of the three Abrahamic religions regard a small patch of ground in Jerusalem as one of its holiest sites. Sadly, this epicenter of the human spirit is also one of the most hotly contested political locations on the planet.

SACRED SPACE: Jews call this site in East Jerusalem Temple Mount; it is home to the Western Wall, the last remnant of the foundation of Judaism's Second Temple. Christians worship here at the Church of the Holy Sepulchre, where the crucified Christ is said to have been laid. Muslims revere the site of the al-Aqsa Mosque, where an angel is said to have given Muhammad a vision of heaven

The Splendor of Islam

Bursting from its birthplace on the Arabian peninsula, Islam swept across the Middle East after the death of its founder and Prophet, Muhammad, in A.D. 632. Within only a few centuries, the world of Islam stretched from Spain in the west to India in the east. In those days of their foremost glory, Muslims led the civilized world in arts and sciences, and such great cities as Baghdad, Cairo and Damascus flowered with poets and artisans, mosques and minarets.

JOURNEY'S END: All Muslims are enjoined to make a pilgrimage, or *hajj*, to Mecca, where they perform a ritual circumambulation, or *tawaf*, of Islam's most sacred site, the Kaaba. This ancient shrine predates Islam; it was filled with pagan idols in the time of Muhammad, which he banished

A First Clash of Cultures

For centuries, while Europe languished in the Dark Ages, Muslim scholars, artists, astronomers and mathematicians flourished. But as Europeans emerged from their long stagnation, their renascent energies found direction across the Mediterranean. The liberation of the historic sites of Christianity from Muslim hands was a sacred duty: "God wills it!" A series of long, bloody, often inconclusive Crusades followed, and the scars of dishonor they left on the Islamic world have never faded away. Even today, al-Qaeda kingpin Osama bin Laden refers to U.S. and European leaders as "Crusaders."

STRONGHOLD: Krac de Chavaliers ("Fortress of the Knights") in Syria was built by the Knights Hospitaliers in A.D. 1031 and expanded in the mid-12th century. At right, a French illustrated manuscript shows Europeans besieging Antioch in the First Crusade in A.D. 1098

A Great War Creates A New Middle East

After the Crusades, the Muslim world entered a long period of decline; by the end of the 19th century, most of the lands of the Middle East were in the fading grip of the Ottoman Empire. When the Ottoman Turks took the losing side in World War I, a new map of the area was created by victorious Britain and France, and many of the nations that emerged—Iraq, Kuwait, Palestine and others—were creations of European political necessity, often bearing little or no resemblance to the diverse cultures, religions and loyalties of their inhabitants. The result was a recipe for anger and instability.

FISH OUT OF WATER: British soldiers and Bedouins teamed up to fight the Central Powers in World War I; this picture was taken in 1917

Birth of a Nation

From the shattering wreckage of World War II and the terrible Nazi Holocaust, a new nation was born: Israel. The new homeland fulfilled the dream of a people long scattered in the Diaspora, but from the moment of its creation it has been despised by its Arab neighbors. Refusing to recognize Israel's right to exist—or to accept the U.N.'s promised homeland for the displaced native Palestinians—Arab nations have waged a constant struggle against "the Zionist entity." And the plight of the Palestinian refugees has made peace a stranger to the modern Middle East.

TWO PEOPLES: Left, survivors of the Buchenwald death camp arrive in Palestine in 1945. Below, a Palestinian refugee camp in Lebanon in 1955

A New Age of Oil

Remote, self-contained and set apart from the West by its languages, customs and religions, the Middle East remained aloof from world affairs for centuries. But that insularity was shattered by a quirk of geography: its desert sands concealed vast deposits of the single most important commodity of the 20th century, oil. Within decades of this discovery, the Middle East was utterly transformed. Its relationship with a newly dependent Western world has left its peoples far wealthier and much more involved in global politics than ever before but also unmoored from their past and often unsure of their place in the modern world.

FLOATING WEALTH: A supertanker makes port at Ras Tanurah, site of major oil refineries on Saudi Arabia's Persian Gulf coast, near one of the world's richest reservoirs of petroleum

The Rise of Islamism

The appearance of Israel in the Middle East gave Arab inhabitants something they hadn't had for centuries: a common enemy. Anger and anti-Semitism were a toxic brew, especially when blended with the sense of cultural displacement caused by a rapid, oil-fueled collision with the modern West. Soon an unlikely batch of leaders— Arab nationalists, Palestinian guerrillas, fundamentalist mullahs and academics, West-hating terrorists—created a powerfully appealing new movement in the Muslim world: militant Islamism.

MOBILIZING: Members of the Palestinian militia and political group Hamas march in a 2001 procession honoring a suicide bomber

Stuck in the Middle

Tiny Lebanon is a bit player in Middle East politics, trapped between the garrison state of Israel and the aggressively anti-Israeli nations of Syria and Iran. Lebanon's government has for decades been dominated by Syrian strongmen, who channel money and guns to the militia group Hizballah, which has become embedded in the nation's political life. When Hizballah fighters kidnapped two Israeli soldiers in July 2006, the incident touched off a major war—and the capital city of Beirut, recently restored to sparkling life after a civil war that lasted from 1975 to 1990—was once again splintered into shards.

MORE WAR: Lebanese men react on July 14, 2006, as Beirut's Rafik Hariri International Airport is bombed by Israeli aircraft

The World Of Islam

For centuries the dominant religion in the Middle East, Islam is rapidly gaining new followers around the world

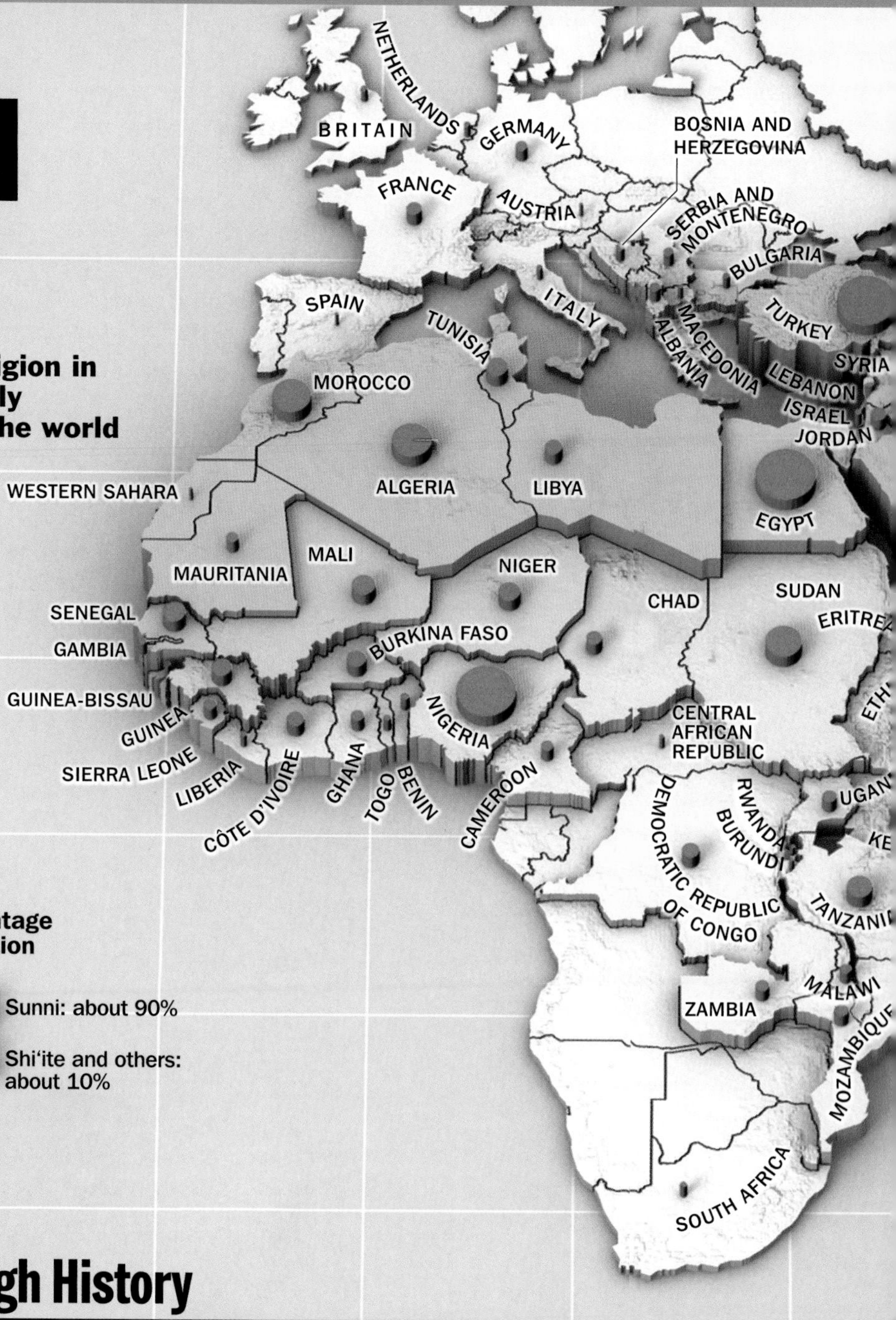

BRITAIN
NETHERLANDS
GERMANY
BOSNIA AND HERZEGOVINA
FRANCE
AUSTRIA
SERBIA AND MONTENEGRO
BULGARIA
SPAIN
ITALY
MACEDONIA
ALBANIA
TURKEY
TUNISIA
SYRIA
LEBANON
ISRAEL
JORDAN
MOROCCO
ALGERIA
LIBYA
EGYPT
WESTERN SAHARA
MAURITANIA
MALI
NIGER
CHAD
SUDAN
ERITREA
SENEGAL
GAMBIA
BURKINA FASO
GUINEA-BISSAU
GUINEA
SIERRA LEONE
LIBERIA
CÔTE D'IVOIRE
GHANA
TOGO
BENIN
NIGERIA
CAMEROON
CENTRAL AFRICAN REPUBLIC
DEMOCRATIC REPUBLIC OF CONGO
RWANDA
BURUNDI
TANZANIA
MALAWI
ZAMBIA
MOZAMBIQUE
SOUTH AFRICA

Muslims in the Americas

Of the world's 1.5 billion Muslims, only a small percentage live in the Americas, but that number is increasing rapidly. The American Religious Identification Survey, taken in 2001, showed 1.1 million Muslims living in the U.S., accounting for .05% of the total population.

Muslim sects as a percentage of world Muslim population

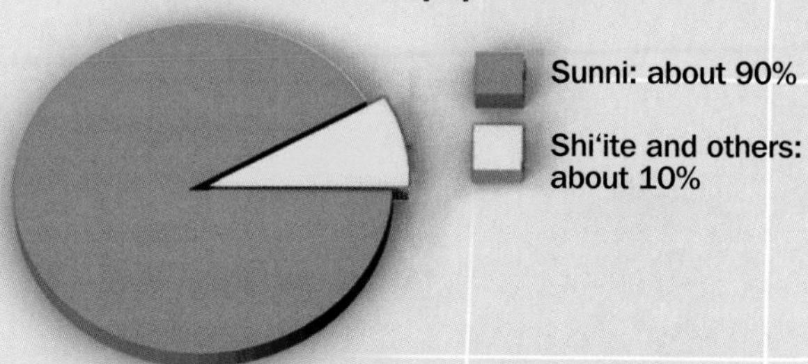

Sunni: about 90%
Shi'ite and others: about 10%

The Middle East Through History

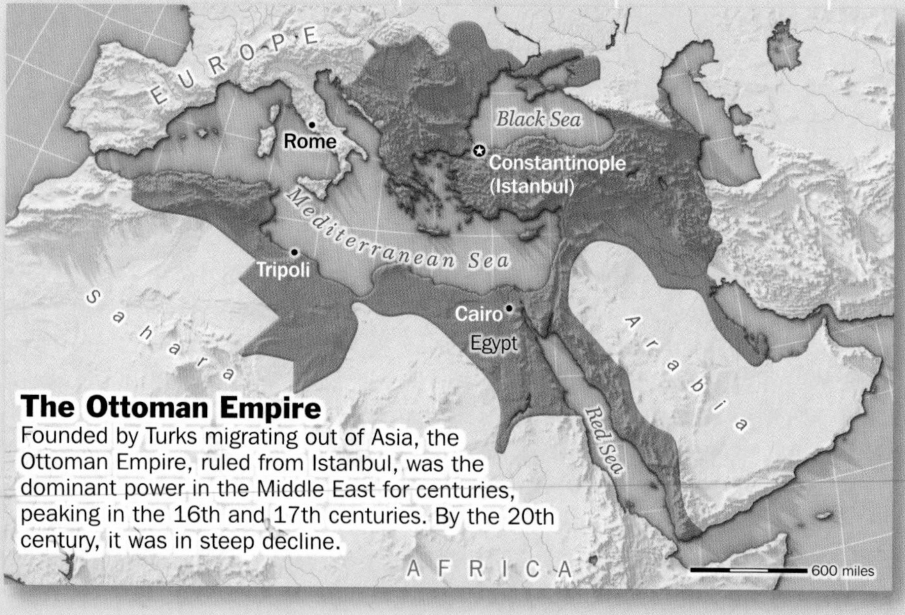

EUROPE
Rome
Black Sea
Constantinople (Istanbul)
Mediterranean Sea
Tripoli
Sahara
Cairo
Egypt
Arabia
Red Sea
AFRICA
600 miles

The Ottoman Empire

Founded by Turks migrating out of Asia, the Ottoman Empire, ruled from Istanbul, was the dominant power in the Middle East for centuries, peaking in the 16th and 17th centuries. By the 20th century, it was in steep decline.

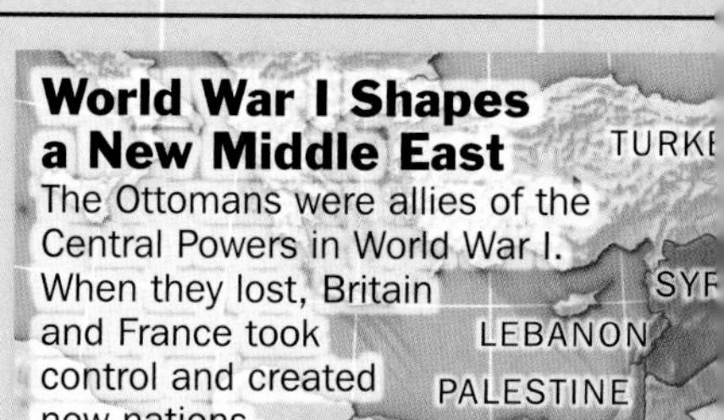

TURKE
SYR
LEBANON
PALESTINE
EGYPT
New nations under French control
New nations under British control
Areas under British mandate before 1914

World War I Shapes a New Middle East

The Ottomans were allies of the Central Powers in World War I. When they lost, Britain and France took control and created new nations, which did not reflect local cultures.

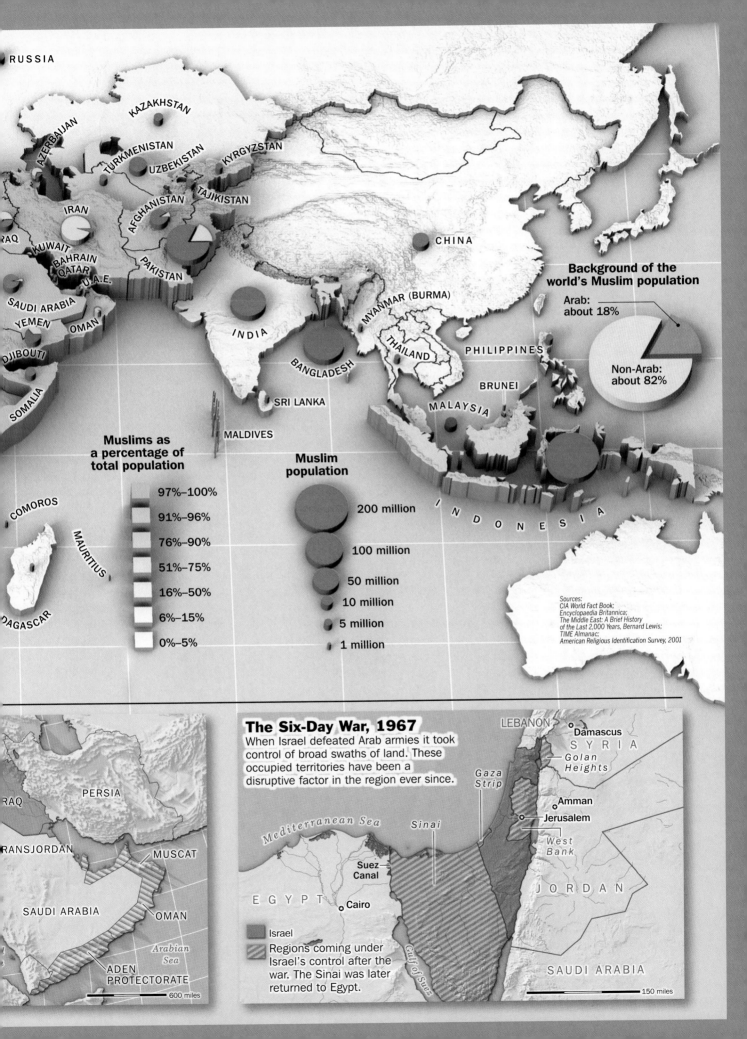

RUSSIA

KAZAKHSTAN

AZERBAIJAN
TURKMENISTAN
UZBEKISTAN
KYRGYZSTAN
TAJIKISTAN
AFGHANISTAN
IRAN
IRAQ
KUWAIT
BAHRAIN
QATAR
U.A.E.
PAKISTAN
SAUDI ARABIA
YEMEN
OMAN
DJIBOUTI
SOMALIA

CHINA

INDIA

MYANMAR (BURMA)

BANGLADESH

THAILAND

PHILIPPINES

SRI LANKA

MALDIVES

BRUNEI

MALAYSIA

INDONESIA

COMOROS

MAURITIUS

MADAGASCAR

Background of the world's Muslim population

Arab: about 18%

Non-Arab: about 82%

Muslims as a percentage of total population

- 97%–100%
- 91%–96%
- 76%–90%
- 51%–75%
- 16%–50%
- 6%–15%
- 0%–5%

Muslim population

- 200 million
- 100 million
- 50 million
- 10 million
- 5 million
- 1 million

Sources:
CIA World Fact Book;
Encyclopaedia Britannica;
The Middle East: A Brief History
of the Last 2,000 Years, Bernard Lewis;
TIME Almanac;
American Religious Identification Survey, 2001

The Six-Day War, 1967

When Israel defeated Arab armies it took control of broad swaths of land. These occupied territories have been a disruptive factor in the region ever since.

IRAQ
PERSIA
TRANSJORDAN
MUSCAT
SAUDI ARABIA
OMAN
Arabian Sea
ADEN PROTECTORATE

600 miles

LEBANON

Damascus
SYRIA
Golan Heights

Gaza Strip

Mediterranean Sea

Sinai

Amman
Jerusalem

West Bank

Suez Canal

EGYPT

Cairo

JORDAN

Gulf of Suez

■ Israel

▨ Regions coming under Israel's control after the war. The Sinai was later returned to Egypt.

SAUDI ARABIA

150 miles

Who's Who in the Middle East

Osama bin Laden

Mahmoud Abbas Yasser Arafat's successor and President of the Palestinian Authority since 2005, he is a moderate who has inspired a measure of trust from Israelis. He is at odds with the militant Hamas Party.

Abdullah bin Abdulaziz Absolute monarch of Saudi Arabia since August 2005, he is a pro-Western moderate often regarded as a transitional figure, owing to his advanced age: he was 81 at the time of his accession.

Abdullah II Jordan's King since 1999, he has improved the economy and strengthened ties to the West but also clamped down on dissent at home.

Mahmoud Ahmadinejad President of Iran. Both hard-liner and populist, the former mayor of Tehran was elected in 2005. Although he has little actual power, he has stirred controversy, saying Israel should be "wiped off the map" and refusing to stop enriching uranium.

Yasser Arafat (1929–2004) The long-time chairman of the P.L.O. and the first President of the Palestinian Authority, he sponsored terrorism and embodied his people's aspirations, but

his greatest single talent may have been for survival.

Bashar Assad The President of Syria since 2004 was trained in ophthalmology but was catapulted into power when his father's first son died in a 1994 car crash. The accidental autocrat succeeded his late father in 2000.

Hafez Assad (1930–2000) The late President of Syria was a fighter pilot who took power in 1971 and brought stability to a country long plagued by upheavals. The price: he presided over a brutally repressive regime.

Mustafa Kemal Ataturk (1881–1938) Turkey's former President dragged the nation he forged from the ruins of the Ottoman Empire into the 20th century.

Ehud Barak Former PM of Israel, he saw his peacemaking dreams die in 2000, when negotiations for a comprehensive peace between Israel and the Palestinians foundered on the status of Jerusalem and the "right of return."

David Ben-Gurion (1886–1973) Israel's George Washington was the first PM of the new Jewish state, the architect of its relationship with the U.S. and an advocate for returning territory after the 1967 Six-Day War.

Recep Tayyip Erdogan Turkey's PM since 2003 is a devout Muslim who has moved his nation steadily closer to member ship in the E.U.

Muammar Gaddafi Libya's ruler since 1969 was an advocate of Arab nationalism and a major sponsor of terrorism but is now a law-abiding member of the international community.

Ismail Haniya The leader of Hamas and PM of the Palestinian Authority since 2006 was born in a Gaza refugee camp and survived at least one Israeli assassination attempt. He advocates maximum confrontation and minimum accommodation with the Jewish state.

Rafik Hariri (1944–2005) The billionaire businessmen and former PM helped lead Lebanon's rebirth (and finance its rebuilding) after a 15-year civil war. Widespread fury at the presumed involvement of Damascus in his 2005 murder ended decades of Syrian occupation in Lebanon.

Hussein The late King of Jordan, a perennial tightrope walker, balanced friendly relations with the West against the needs of Arab nationalism. In the first Gulf War, he tilted toward Saddam Hussein's Iraq, yet in 1994 he led Jordan to become the second Arab state to make peace with Israel, after Egypt.

Hamid Karzai Afghanistan's President and a provincial Afghan tribal prince backed by the West, he is fighting to gain control over his vast land, where regional warlords have long held sway.

Ayatullah Ali Khamenei Iran's Supreme Leader, the successor to Ayatullah Ruhollah Khomeini, staunchly espouses his mentor's militant interpretation of Shi'ite Islam and opposes reform. But some Western observers believe he is a relative (if quiet) moderate who doesn't seek confrontation.

Ayatullah Ruhollah Khomeini (1900?–1989) The dour cleric who led the 1979

T.E. Lawrence

Islamic revolution in Iran perceived himself above all as an avenger of the perceived humiliations that the West had inflicted on the Muslims of the Middle East. His war with the West consisted mostly of words, but his eight-year reckoning with Saddam Hussein cost millions lives.

Osama bin Laden The leader and co-founder of al-Qaeda and mastermind of a series of terrorist attacks on the U.S., including 9/11, was reported in the autumn of 2006 to be seriously ill and near death. The Saudi fundamentalist's record is secure: no terrorist has ever done more damage, and none has ever held a more hypnotic appeal for angry Muslims.

T.E. Lawrence (1888-1935) "Lawrence of Arabia" didn't invent regime change, but nobody was ever better at it. A Briitsh spy who traveled in the guise of an archaeologist, he persuaded restive tribal chiefs to revolt against Ottoman rule in World War I. He helped win the regional war but felt his nation later betrayed the Arabs.

Nouri al-Maliki Iraq's Prime Minister since the spring of 2006 emerged as a compromise candidate only after the first choice of his Shi'ite faction, former Prime Minister Ibrahim al-Jaafari, was vetoed by Sunni and Kurd groups. Critics fear that al-Maliki has stronger ties to Tehran than to Washington.

Hosni Mubarak The President of Egypt is its longest-serving ruler in more than a century. Willing to suppress dissent brutally, he has officially banned the fundamentalist Muslim Brotherhood, which is enormously popular. Egypt under Mubarak is a democracy in the Middle Eastern style: he has scored lopsided victories in every election, and his son may succeed him.

Pervez Musharraf Pakistan's ruler since 1999 (and President since 2001) was unaligned before 9/11 but has been

Mahmoud Ahmadinejad

a U.S. ally in the fight against the Taliban, although he faces strong internal opposition to that policy. Critics in the West charge his support is halfhearted.

Hassan Nasrallah Hizballah leader since 1991 and smoother and more media savvy than other anti-U.S. Arab leaders, he lured Israel into a major campaign against his militant group in the summer of 2006. By surviving, he made himself a hero of the Arab street.

Gamal Abdel Nasser (1918-1970) Egypt's fiery president was the foremost proponent of pan-Arabism and a modernizer of his nation. He hurled his armies against Israel but never succeeded in defeating it.

Benjamin Netanyahu Israel's PM from 1996 to 1999 was eclipsed by a fellow conservative and hawk, Ariel Sharon, until the latter bolted from the Likud Party to form the centrist Kadima Party and suffered a debilitating stroke. Netanyahu is now the heir apparent to the leadership of the Israeli right.

Ehud Olmert The acting PM of Israel following the January 2006 stroke that felled Ariel Sharon was elected in his own right two months later. He lacks both the personal charisma and military credentials of his mentor, Sharon. His robust response to Hizballah provocation sent Israeli troops into Lebanon in 2006, but ended with Hizballah's survival and his popularity in a tailspin.

Saddam Hussein The remorseless Sunni Muslim tyrant whose Baath Party ruled Iraq for a quarter-century killed domestic opponents by the hundreds of thousands and foreign enemies by the millions. Facing trial under a new, U.S.-installed regime, he is unrepentant.

Fouad Siniora The Prime Minister of Lebanon since 2005 is a Sunni Muslim and close ally of the late Rafik Hariri. A pro-West technocrat, he leads a relatively weak government in a nation long dominated by Syria and filled with Hizballah supporters.

Grand Ayatullah Ali Husaini Sistani One of only five living Grand Ayatullahs in the world, he is the most senior Shi'ite cleric in Iraq. Since the 2003 U.S. invasion, he has followed a moderate line. His chief rival is upstart cleric Muqtada al-Sadr.

Ahmed Yassin (1937-2004) The founder and spiritual leader of Hamas was assassinated by rockets from an Israeli helicopter in 2004. Nearly blind and a quadriplegic since childhood, the charismatic cleric nonetheless ordered and orchestrated suicide bombings that killed hundreds of Israelis. ■

Gamal Abdel Nasser

Glossary of Terms

Dome of the Rock

Aliyah Jewish immigration to Palestine and/or Israel; promoted by Zionists.

Allah God; the Arabic term for Lord. Islam's most basic profession of faith is, "There is but one God [Allah], and Muhammad is his Prophet."

Ayatullah "Sign of God," a term of high clerical rank in Shi'ite Islam.

Baath Party A major political party in Syria and Iraq, it espouses secular nationalism, pan-Arabism and socialism; the party of Saddam Hussein.

Balfour Declaration The 1917 commitment by Britain to support the cause of a Jewish homeland in Palestine.

Bedouin An Arab nomad of the desert.

British Mandate of Palestine Granted by the League of Nations following World War I, it gave Britain control over the governance of Palestine.

burqa The head-to-toe garment, often blue, worn by Islamic women, primarily in Afghanistan; required daily wear for all women when the Taliban ruled the nation.

Caliph A successor; in the Sunni tradition the term was applied to the clerics who succeeded Muhammad after his death; Islam's highest clerical position.

Dome of the Rock Sometimes called the Mosque of Umar, the third holiest site in Islam is located in the Noble Sanctuary, the sacred complex in the Old City of Jerusalem.

emir A title of high office in the secular realm; a ruler or leader.

Fatah Once the most extreme wing of the P.L.O., Fatah now represents the moderate center; the party of Yasser Arafat and Mahmoud Abbas.

fatwa A legal ruling; more widely used to describe a death sentence issued by a cleric against one who has violated Shari'a.

Hadith A concordance of writings and commentaries that supplements Islam's holiest book, the Koran.

hajj The pilgrimage to Mecca every adult Muslim male is encouraged to make in his lifetime.

Hamas Originally a violent group of Palestinian militants, it evolved to offering social services and is now a political party that controls the Palestinian Authority legislature.

Hizballah Militant Lebanese group long associated with terrorist raids against Israel. Led by Sheik Hassan Nasrallah and supported by Syria and Iran, it has become a dominant political and social force in its nation.

imam Arabic for leader; generally, but not always, applied to clerics, particularly in the Shi'ite sect of Islam.

intifadeh An uprising; used specifically to refer to rebellions against Israeli rule by Palestinians in the occupied territories beginning in 1987.

Islamic Jihad Militant group based in Syria; its most prominent offshoot is Palestinian Islamic Jihad, led by Sheik Abdullah Ramadan.

Islamist One who believes Islam is the one true religion and must prevail over all others; a fundamentalist who seeks Islam's return to an idealized past.

jihad A holy war, or more broadly, a struggle of any kind, as performed by a jihadist, or holy warrior.

Kaaba Islam's central shrine, at Mecca; end destination of the hajj pilgrimage

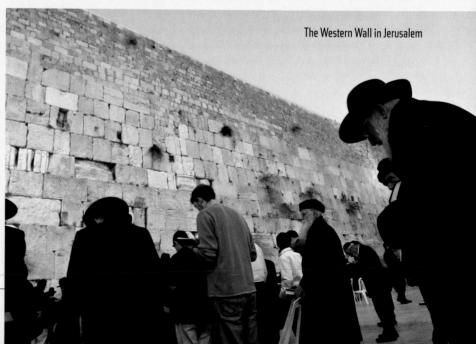

The Western Wall in Jerusalem

Members of Palestinian Islamic Jihad

made by millions each year.

keffiyeh Black-and-white checked scarf worn by Palestinians.

Koran Islam's sacred book was dictated by the Angel Gabriel to Muhammad; its study and memorization remain central to practice of the faith.

madrasah An Islamic school; religious instruction is often stressed.

Mahdi Army Militia force created by Iraqi Shi'ite cleric Muqtada al-Sadr; it led the first major confrontation with U.S. forces occupying Iraq in 2004.

Mecca Islam's most sacred city is the birthplace of Muhammad; home of the faith's most revered shrine, the Kaaba; and site of the ritual pilgrimage, the hajj.

Medina Sacred city on the Arabian Peninsula, where Muhammad sought refuge after fleeing Mecca.

mosque The basic house of worship in Islam, with its central space usually divided by gender. More elaborate mosques boast minarets, slender spires that are perches for muezzins.

muezzin A cleric who summons the faithful to pray five times each day from the minaret of a mosque.

mujahedin Afghan guerrillas who fought the Soviet invasion of the 1980s; the singular is *mujahid*.

mullah An Islamic clergyman, most commonly in the Shi'ite sect.

Muslim Brotherhood A strongly militant Islamist group founded in Egypt in 1928; it is currently outlawed there and in several other Arab nations.

occupied territories The Arab lands taken over by Israel following the Six-Day War; a constant source of irritation in the Middle East.

Ottoman Empire The Turks ruled much of the Middle East for centuries, roughly from the 1200s to 1919, when the empire fell following World War I.

Palestine Liberation Organization/ Palestine Authority A longtime militant group fighting for Palestinian rights, often through terrorist tactics, the P.L.O. was transformed into the politically respectable Palestinian Authority following the 1993 Oslo Accords. It now manages the semi-autonomous Palestinian territories within Israel.

Pan-Arabism Memorably espoused by Egypt's former leader Gamal Abdel Nasser, it is the drive to unite all Arabs in a single political entity.

Ramadan The annual holy month on the Islamic calendar, it is a time of daily fasting and denial—and nightly feasts.

Right of Return The term used by Palestinians to describe their demand to reclaim the lands they lost in the 1948 birth of the state of Israel; a perennial sticking point in attempts to resolve the Palestinian-Israeli conflict.

Shari'a The Islamic law is deeply rooted in the teachings of Muhammad and widely applied across the Middle East.

Sunni The majority branch of Islam. Its believers, who tend to be of higher social status than the rival Shi'ites, claim to follow Muhammad's original teachings.

Sykes–Picot Agreement A 1916 secret pact between Britain and France, it divvied up the lands of the Ottoman Empire following World War I.

Wahhabism A fundamental, reformist strain in Islam founded by Muhammad ibn 'Abddul al-Wahhab in 1745. It is growing in popularity amid the current Islamist revival.

Western Wall Judaism's most sacred site, it is the last remnant of the foundation wall of the Second Temple. It is located in the Old City of Jerusalem, near Islam's Noble Sanctuary.

United Nations Resolution 242 Passed in 1967, it called on Israel to return the Arab lands it occupied after the Six-Day War and return to the boundaries that existed prior to the conflict.

Zionism European movement that championed the return of Jews scattered in the Diaspora to Palestine, where they hoped to found a new nation of Israel.

An Afghan woman in a burqa

The Peoples, Places and Faiths of the Middle East

The Middle East is home to a broad diversity of peoples: Persians and Turks, Bedouins and Kurds, Sunnis and Shi'ites. Two great cultural forces unite many of them. The first is the religion of Islam, which has dominated these lands for 1,300 years. The second is the Arabic language: Arabs define themselves as those who speak this tongue in which Islam's holy book, the Koran, is written. Turks, Jews, Iranians and others who don't speak Arabic are thus distinct cultures. Look closer, and more diversity appears: in this vast crescent of countries there is a dazzling mosaic of nations, races, sects, languages—and dreams.

The Koran

Non-Muslims often misunderstand, and almost always underestimate, the importance Islam attaches to the Koran (in Arabic, "Recitation"): it is the centerpiece of this most literate of religious cultures. In a faith without priests and so opposed to idolatry that it prohibits not only images of God but also most figurative representations of any kind, the words of the Koran—their physical manifestation in the book—represent God's presence in this world. Muslims believe that the Koran was not created but has existed with God for all eternity.

The Koran is complemented by the Hadith, a collection of sermons, oral lessons and commentaries that illuminate the Koran's message.

Islam, Judaism and Christianity

Muslims regard Abraham, left, as a major prophet. Muhammad said his message was but a restoration of Abrahamic faith, and the Koran advises Muslims proselytized by either Jews or Christians to answer, "Nay … we follow the religion of Abraham." Muslims also regard Jesus as sacred but entirely human and one of God's "messengers" (great prophets), rather than the embodiment of God.

The Paradox of Islam

"I N THE NAME OF THE ONE GOD, THE Compassionate One, the Merciful One," begins the Koran, Islam's founding document and holy book. Those words galvanized the Middle East when they were first set on paper in the 7th century A.D. Within a century of Islam's founding, the new faith spread throughout the Middle East. In another 200 years, it had taken root as far away as the countries we now know as Spain and India. Today, with 1.5 billion adherents worldwide, Islam is the world's second largest religion—although many Americans are surprised to learn that fully 80% of the faithful live outside the Arab world.

Much of Islam's growth was achieved at the point of a sword, and from the first, Islam's adherents won fame for ferocious courage in combat. In the wake of their conquests, however, Islamic rulers also earned a reputation, often forgotten today, for tolerance and moderation; they treated Christians, Jews and others in their midst with respect. Indeed, much of Islam's intolerance has been reserved for its own: in the first century of the Muslim era, the religion cleaved into two major sects, the Sunnis and the Shi'ites, and the wounds have never healed.

It is this respect and tolerance for others that seem to have gone missing in the great fundamentalist revival that has swept across the Islamic world, especially in Arab lands, in recent years. Western observers have christened this extreme form of the religion Islamism. It insists that all humans must submit to the will of Muhammad's God, and that believ-

don't share their beliefs. From this thinking sprang the terrorist attacks of 9/11 and a litany of lesser horrors.

It's true that Islamist terrorists make up a small minority of the Arab world and an even tinier fraction of the global Muslim world. But while their hideous deeds resound everywhere, a troubling silence persists. Where are the voices of Islam's moderate clerics and scholars, denouncing terrorism as the perversion of a great religion?

ONE HINT: THE SECULARISM OF Western states is alien to Islam. Shari'a, Islamic law, provides guidance for all aspects of Muslim life—public and private, devotional and secular, civil and criminal. The separation of church and state strikes many Muslims as unnatural, sacrilegious. For this reason, Muslim countries with secular governments, like Egypt and Turkey, often float atop deep reservoirs of instability, as religious voices call for more control.

The word Islam means "submission" (to the will of God). For many in the West, the central paradox of Islam today rests in the dichotomy between what it preaches—submission to one loving God and respect and tolerance for others—and what it practices: tolerance for those who

Five Pillars of Islam

The core of Islamic faith, especially for Sunnis, is summed up by these five practices:

1. The *shahada*, or profession of faith: "There is no god but God; Muhammad is the Prophet of God." Every Muslim must recite the profession aloud at least once in his lifetime. It confers membership in the *ummah*, or Muslim community.

2. The five daily prayers: These are made at dawn, midday, mid-afternoon, sunset and before retiring. The more devout kneel and face Mecca. Prayer is believed to be more effective if done collectively and when performed on Fridays.

3. *Zakat*, or alms giving: Every Muslim is expected to donate a portion of his wealth to charity each year.

4. The Ramadan fast: For an entire lunar month, Muslims refrain from food, drink, tobacco and sex between sunrise and sunset. Ramadan is considered a period of heightened spirituality.

5. The hajj, or pilgrimage to Mecca: The journey takes place annually during the last month of the Muslim year. It is an obligation for every Muslim to make the hajj at least once, provided he is physically and financially able to do so.

The Life of Muhammad

Recite!" a mysterious voice commanded the young man. Muhammad, a humble shepherd who could neither read nor write but was known for being virtuous, had developed the habit of retreating to a cave outside his native town of Mecca to meditate. In this cave a disembodied voice (which later identified itself as the angel Gabriel) commanded him to begin reciting verses, which the angel imparted, saying they were commandments from God. The words Muhammad committed to memory, astonishingly beautiful verses of poetry, became the Koran.

When Muhammad shared the commands he was given, including the injunction to believe only in a single God, Allah, he was initially laughed at, then persecuted. Mecca's economy was based on pilgrimages to the polytheistic shrines located there, and any threat to that revenue was deemed a danger to the community. In fear of their lives, Muhammad and a small group of followers escaped to nearby Medina in the journey known as the hejira. Surrounded there by foes from Mecca, Muhammad led the faithful to miraculous victories against vastly superior numbers. After eight years in exile, he led his followers back to Mecca, where he took control without bloodshed.

Within a few decades, the religion Muhammad founded—Islam—had come to dominate the Arabian peninsula. Within a century of the Prophet's death in A.D. 632, it would spread throughout the Middle East and as far away as Europe and India.

AWAKENING: The Sultan Salahuddin Abdul Aziz Shah mosque in Shah Alam, Malaysia, takes shape at dawn

NOW AND THEN: A man in a Baghdad mosque stands between posters of prominent contemporary Shi'ite cleric Muqtada al-Sadr, left, and the founder of Shi'ism, Imam Ali, the Fourth Caliph

Division of the Faithful

AT THE HEIGHT OF HIS POWER AS a spiritual and political leader, Muhammad died suddenly in A.D. 632, in his early 60s. Long pre-occupied with prophecy and conquest, he left no clear instructions concerning a successor. Even during the Prophet's lifetime, a fissure had begun to appear between his first followers, citizens of Mecca, and his later converts, from Medina. As long as Muhammad was alive, his enormous moral authority bridged the gap. But with his death the schism widened, and zealots on both sides claimed to inherit his mantle.

Abu Bakr, the Prophet's father-in-law, was chosen as the interim leader and accepted by nearly all Muhammad's followers; he became known as the First Caliph (Arabic for successor). But when Bakr died of natural causes only two years later, the arguments began anew. With the First Caliph gone, the supporters of Ali, Muhammad's cousin, son-in-law and leader of the Medina faction, were sure that their turn had come. For Ali was among those passed over in favor of Bakr. They were wrong: two

more Caliphs followed Bakr, ruling for another 22 years. When the Third Caliph was assassinated in 656 (as the Second Caliph had been, in 644), Ali finally took power. But Muawiyah, the governor of the territory we now call Syria, was related to Ali's murdered predecessor and refused to accept the Fourth Caliph's legitimacy. The civil war, brewing for two decades, finally erupted. Ali moved his sect to Iraq, where he was assassinated in A.D. 661.

The governor of Syria now proclaimed himself the new Caliph, but Ali's followers would never again conform for the sake of Islamic unity. Calling themselves *Shiat Ali* ("Partisans of Ali"), they broke off into the separate branch of Islam we now know as the Shi'ites. The mainstream group from which they broke away considers itself the custodian of the faith's authentic tradition, or *sunnah;* its followers are the Sunnis.

Now, as then, the vast majority of Muslims, more than 80%, are Sunnis. They tend to embrace worldly success as a sign of Allah's favor. Shi'ites, who believe Ali was cheated of his

birthright and then murdered, view dispossession and humiliation as badges of honor. They also have a long-standing preoccupation with martyrdom derived from the end met by each of their leaders, or Imams: after Ali's murder, a succession of 11 Imams all died violently over the next 300 years. The 12th, known as the Mahdi, mysteriously disappeared in the 9th century. Shi'ites believe he will reappear at the end of the world as their redeemer.

There is an element of a class system in Islam's divided house. Broadly speaking, Sunnis are more likely than Shi'ites to be well educated, to fill top positions in government and to be academics and professionals. Many Sunnis disdain Shi'ites as society's lower orders. For centuries, this mutual enmity has fueled unrest and civil wars, as it threatens to do in occupied Iraq in 2006. In that country, Shi'ites are a rare majority of the population, but Saddam Hussein and his colleagues in the ruling Baath Party were Sunnis; they discriminated against Iraq's Shi'ites for decades. Now, for Iraq's underdogs, it's payback time. ■

Women in Islam

WHEN ISLAM SWEPT ACROSS the Middle East in the 7th century, it profoundly changed the place of women in Arab society—for the better. At a time and in a place where women were generally regarded as slightly less valuable than livestock and infant girls were routinely buried alive, Islam outlawed female infanticide, made the education of girls a sacred duty and established a woman's right to own and inherit property. Muhammad even decreed that sexual satisfaction was a woman's entitlement.

Yet although Islam regards women as sacred, it clearly does not regard them as equal to men. As decreed by the Koran, men are entitled to four spouses, whereas women can have only one. Under Shari'a, the value of a woman's testimony in court is worth half that of a man's—and financial compensation to survivors for the murder of a woman is half the going rate for men. The eclipse of Arab women in the Islamic world was in part a reaction to Western expansionism in the 18th and 19th centuries. Fearing cultural erosion, emerging conservative sects championed values that set Islam apart, including the repression of women.

WHILE IT IS IMPOSSIBLE, GIVEN THEIR diversity, to paint a single picture of women living under Islam today, it is clear that inequality is deeply entrenched in many Muslim countries. Wives in Islamic societies face great difficulty in suing for divorce, but husbands can be released from their vows virtually on demand.

Fear of poverty keeps many Muslim women locked in bad marriages, as does the prospect of losing their children. Typically, fathers win custody of boys over the age of 6 and girls after the onset of puberty. Wife beating is prevalent in the Muslim world, and each year hundreds of Muslim women die in "honor killings"—murders by husbands or male relatives of women suspected of disobedience, usually a sexual indiscretion. Typically, the killers are punished lightly, if at all. Many Muslims respond to criticism of such matters by pointing out that crime rates are low and pornography illegal in most Islamic nations, while sexual exploitation in commerce and entertainment is almost nonexistent.

Patriarchal traditions are slowly declining in some areas. In recent years, hereditary rulers in five gulf states have named women to Cabinet posts for the first time; in Kuwait and Oman women can now vote. Local culture also shapes roles. In many Arab countries tradition keeps most women at home and off the street, but in Persian Iran, women enjoy much more liberty: they drive cars, buy property, own businesses, vote and hold public office and crowd Tehran's avenues day and night.

The last word belongs to the women themselves, and many of them say they find liberation in their faith. The veil that is mandated by Islamic tradition (and required by law in many Arab countries) may seem a symbol of oppression to the Western eye, but to many women who wear it, it represents freedom from unwanted sexual advances as well as pride in Islam. ∎

REBEL: Among heavily veiled Afghan peers at the Blue Mosque in Mazar-e-Sharif in 2002, one woman dares to expose her face and hair

The Terrorists

IN THE MIDDLE EAST, TERRORISTS come in a wide variety of shades and stripes, but they generally fall into two categories: those who are trying to claim for themselves a place at the table where nations confer and human fates are decided—and those who just want to blow up the table.

The terrorist groups that dominated the headlines in the 1970s and early '80s almost always fell into the first category. The Palestine Liberation Organization, Black September and others—not unlike the Jewish terrorists who fought against British rule in Palestine in the 1940s—were trying to achieve specific goals, as limited as the release of prisoners and as broad as the destruction of Israel. Those militias were generally secular and much more political than religious in orientation. The homicidal attacks they staged were often designed to capture world attention for their cause rather than to kill large numbers of innocent people.

There was generally a sense of transaction in their operations: if our demands are met (say, by providing us with a plane to fly to Jordan), we will respond as promised (by releasing hostages, for example). If they are not, we will react by executing hostages and staging more attacks.

By the 1990s, however, a new strain of terrorism arose, conducted by religiously inspired groups pursuing theological rather than political ends. Their terrorism is not transactional: instead of taking hostages and making demands, terrorist groups like Osama bin Laden's al-Qaeda often attacked without warning in operations designed for maximum bloodshed. At first, these groups often did not issue communiqués or claim responsibility for attacks. Moreover, tapping into a tradition of suicidal vengeance (particularly in exchange for a posthumous reward) that has deep roots in Arab Islamic culture, al-Qaeda often employed suicide bombers.

This new wave of terrorism is based in Islamist dreams of glory, and that's one reason it is so difficult to fight. Apart from broad injunctions for "Crusaders and Jews" to leave the Holy Land, al-Qaeda has never issued specific demands, nor has it offered to stop its attacks in exchange for a list of concessions. Instead, it has preferred to let its actions speak for themselves.

In this second form of terrorism, each attack serves another goal: it is a recruiting notice for new terrorists. Bin Laden's ultimate goal is far more ambitious than simply knocking down buildings and killing people, and it cannot be summed up by describing him as an evildoer who hates freedom. On a mission from God, bin Laden seeks to rally the Islamic faithful around the world to his ultimate cause: restoring the Ottoman caliphate that was overthrown after World War I by Mustafa Kemal Ataturk in Turkey; ridding the Middle East of Israel and Western influence; spreading Islam across the globe and ushering in a golden age,

POWER: Palestinian militants are framed by burning tires. The Israeli-Palestinian stand-off has been used as a recruiting tool around the Islamic world for decades

the same God he does and worship God in precisely the way he prescribes.

The extent to which bin Laden is succeeding can be measured by the increasing number of terrorist attacks around the world that are not conducted by al-Qaeda but emulate its example. Bin Laden, in one sense, is aiming to make himself superfluous; he seeks to light an Islamist fire that will multiply itself around the globe, espoused by clerics and led by thousands of holy warriors inspired by his words and his works. As he said of the people the West regards as terrorists in a 1999 interview with TIME: Those who sacrifice their lives "to earn the pleasure of God are real men. They managed to rid the Islamic nation of disgrace. We hold them in the highest esteem." ∎

The Palestinian group Hamas and Hizballah in Lebanon are models of political terrorism, staging attacks as part of a strategy designed to achieve pragmatic rather than theological goals. Both Hizballah, which seeks greater power in Lebanon, and Hamas, which now holds partial power in the Palestinian territories, have transformed themselves from their entirely militant origins. Each is also a social agency that operates support facilities for citizens. This metamorphosis is not unusual in the history of militancy. At right is the late Hamas founder Ahmed Yassin.

Freelance Terrorists

Like a stone thrown into a pond, an act of terrorism sends ripples to the wider world. One target: disaffected youths, many of whom see little future in their worlds. They are often recruited by radical clerics, as is believed to have been the case with the London subway

bombers of 2005, left. Some appear to be sponsored by larger terrorist groups: South Asian group Jemaah Islamiah seems to have such a relationship with al-Qaeda. Until a tipping point is reached, when such voices no longer attract the angry, terrorism will not die.

Islamist Terrorists

In a July 2006 videotape, al-Qaeda No. 2 man Ayman al-Zawahiri vowed to recapture every piece of Muslim land "from Spain to Iraq." Al-Qaeda and other Islamist terrorists seek nothing less than a restoration of the Waqf—territory claimed under the Islamic precept that "any land the Muslims have conquered by force" (as parts of Spain were) belongs to them forever, because "the Muslims consecrated these lands to Muslim generations until the Day of Judgment." This stunning vision, most memorably espoused by Osama bin Laden, seeks to reshape the entire world through apocalyptic violence aimed at the West and relegates the Israeli-Palestinian conflict to the status of a sideshow—though it is still a potent fulcrum with which to leverage support among angry Arabs.

Impact of Oil

"EVERYTHING IS SOOTHED BY OIL," wrote the ancient Roman scholar Pliny the Elder, but on this score he was less than prophetic. As the human race's restless search for energy has migrated from wood and wind to coal and whale oil, and finally to petroleum (literally, "rock oil") the stakes and the tension that surround the quest for fuel have risen exponentially.

The history of the 20th century is written in petroleum. Thirsty for oil, European powers carved up the remains of the Ottoman Empire in the years after World War I with an eye toward ensuring their mastery of the Middle East in perpetuity, for even then the region was believed to house the largest repositories of oil on the planet.

The need for oil also sparked World War II. The Japanese attacked Pearl Harbor because, lacking reserves of their own, they needed to conquer the Dutch East Indies but felt safer doing so if they could first score a knockout blow that would frighten the U.S. and Britain into leaving them a free hand in the Pacific. Oil also helped end that global conflict: in 1945, Nazi Germany was still producing plenty of everything it needed to continue fighting the war—except oil.

HISTORICALLY, NATIONS THAT HAVE A vital need for resources they lack (water, wheat, gold, etc.) are very likely to face one of two fates: dominate nations that can supply the need or be dominated by them. For no commodity is this truer than petroleum. As a Shell Oil executive said in TIME's May 4, 1970, issue, this fuel "is seldom found where it is most needed, and seldom most needed where it is found." And the truth is that the big, developed nations that most need petroleum to keep their economies working in high thrum have the least of it.

One exception to this general rule is the U.S., which was both the world's largest producer of oil as well as its single biggest consumer for more than a century, beginning in the 1860s.

By the early 1970s, though, America's demand for gasoline was still rising, even as production leveled off, then began declining. The U.S. now produces about as much oil as it did in the late 1940s and is expected in years ahead to follow the bell curve downward, matching its output from the 1930s, 1920s and so on. This curvaceous crisis is called Hubbert's Peak, after geologist King Hubbert, who predicted it almost to the month in the late 1950s.

For decades, U.S. diplomatic and military strategy have been based on the belief that protecting oil-supply lines from the Middle East is essential to U.S. security; the policy was specifically laid out in the 1980 Carter Doctrine. The strategy has led to fateful decisions, such as the U.S.'s 26 years of support for the regime of the Shah of Iran, that kept the oil flowing—but at a long-term cost that now harms U.S. interests. The Carter Doctrine continues to guide U.S. foreign policy: one of the first goals of U.S. troops in the 2003 Iraq incursion was to secure the oil fields.

THE DEMAND FOR OIL HAS NOT ONLY shaped the foreign policies of its consumers; it has also reshaped the world of its producers in the Middle East. The immense riches that oil confers has also created a host of problems: too-rapid modernization; class inequality; border disputes; the opportunity for rogue states to fund large-scale terrorism.

At the dawn of the 21st century, the world needs oil more than ever before. The rapid industrialization taking place in China and India will only make the demand for oil increase. Until humans create a source of energy to replace it, King Petroleum will continue to irritate, not soothe, the world. Note to Pliny: to err is human.

PETROL PERCH: Poised against the sunset like a muezzin of petroleum, an engineer surveys an oil refinery in Saudi Arabia

World's Largest Proven Reserves of Oil (in billions of barrels)	
Saudi Arabia	264.3
Canada	178.8
Iran	132.5
Iraq	115.0
Kuwait	101.5
United Arab Emirates	97.8
Venezuela	79.7
Russia	60.0
Libya	39.1
Nigeria	35.9

InfoPlease: U.S. Department of Energy

The U.S. and Middle Eastern Oil

The notion that the U.S. is "addicted" to oil from the Middle East is largely a myth. Only around 17% of the petroleum this country consumes originates in the Persian Gulf. But the closely related idea that the U.S. is dangerously dependent on oil that comes from outside its borders is true: of the more than 20 million bbl. of oil that Americans burn through each day (a staggering 25% of the world's total consumption), 12 million bbl. is imported from abroad.

So why does the Middle East so often become the focus of popular anxiety about energy resources? For a reason similar to Willie

Sutton's rationale for robbing banks: that's where the oil is. The aggregate reserves of all the Middle Eastern oil producers amount to more than the known reserves in the rest of the world. So when Americans are worried about their reliance on foreign oil, their eyes turn first to the Middle East.

That can lead to moments of strange political theater, such as the February 2006 speech in which President George W. Bush called for a 75% reduction in oil imports from the Middle East over the next 20 years, without specifying a similar reduction from elsewhere around the globe. That led bewildered officials in several Arab oil-producing states to wonder aloud why their oil was less desirable than petroleum from any other part of the world.

The Christians

MILLIONS OF THE WORLD'S Christians call the Middle East by a different name. To followers of Jesus Christ, it is the Holy Land, the place where the son of God preached and prayed, worked miracles and wonders, was crucified and buried—only to rise from the dead in the Resurrection. In addition to the Muslims and Jews who live there, Christians around the world regard the region as their spiritual home, the nativity site not only of their saviour but also of their religion. They too are stakeholders in these lands, already so diverse in their peoples and their pieties.

Its distinction as Christianity's cradle adds another level of complexity to the dense palimpsest that is the modern Middle East. Reading the *Acts of the Apostles* or the epistles of that tireless traveler and evangelist, St. Paul, modern readers journey through an ancient Middle East, one that bears no signs of Islam, which did not emerge until the 7th century A.D.

The New Testament, Christianity's founding text, tells us that St. Paul experienced the vision that converted him to Christianity on the road to Damascus, that Christ was born in Bethlehem and that he turned water into wine in the town of Cana. So for Christians there is an added measure of sadness when the morning's headlines report that Damascus, now the capital of Syria, is a font of support for terrorism; or that Palestinian terrorists are occupying the Church of the Nativity in Bethlehem, as they did for 39 days in 2002; or that Israeli bombs killed 28 civilians in today's Qana, as occurred on July 30, 2006 (though scholars aren't sure the modern town is the same as the biblical town).

JUST AS THE CLASH BETWEEN MUS-lims and Jews bedevils our times, struggles between Christians and

centuries of the Crusades, when nobles and knights, peasants and children embarked on what they believed was a divine mission to free the sacred sites of the Bible from Muslim hands.

For most modern Westerners, this complicated clash of cultures is the yawn-inducing stuff of history textbooks. But one of the great distinctions between Western and Muslim cultures is that the West prefers to train its gaze on the future, whereas Islam often celebrates an idealized past.

For modern jihadists like Osama bin Laden, the Crusades are as fresh as today's newscasts, an insult to Islam that has never been properly atoned for. It is stunning for Americans to read the text of bin Laden's screeds against the West and find him referring to the leaders of the U.S. and Britain by the term he finds most derogatory: "Crusaders." The sense of shame and anger over deeds committed 900 years ago runs that deep for some modern Muslims.

CHRISTIANITY ISN'T CONFINED TO THE past tense in today's Middle East. An estimated 12 million Christians dwell there today, although in almost every land they occupy, they are a distinct minority, and their numbers are waning, not growing. In 1946, two years before the birth of Israel, 13% of Palestine was Christian; by 2000, the figure for the region was a minuscule 2.1%, half Roman Catholic and half Orthodox.

As militant Islam roils the Middle East, the small groups of Christians find themselves in the cross-hairs: they will not be tolerated in Islamist states. Christians around the world were shocked in 2006, when even in an Afghanistan liberated from Tali-ban rule, a Muslim man who con-verted to Christianity in 1990 faced a death penalty and fled the country. Small wonder that Christians around the world add the fate of the Middle

Benedict and the Muslims

The Crusades may be history, but the world was reminded of the deep suspicions and antagonisms that still exist between Christians and Muslims when Pope Benedict XVI, formerly Joseph Cardinal Ratzinger of Germany, set the Muslim world afire with his comments on Sept. 12, 2006 at the University of Regensburg in his native land.

In a highly academic speech, the Pope quoted a 15th century Byzan-tine emperor who said Muhammad had brought "things only evil and inhuman" to the world. Benedict also questioned the concept of jihad, saying the concept of holy war was unreasonable. The remarks caused an uproar: Roman Catholic churches were burned and an Italian nun in Somalia was killed. The Pope quickly apologized, but Muslim leaders continued to denounce his words.

JOY: Christians celebrate Easter at the Church of the Holy Sepulchre in Jerusalem

Christian Minorities In the Middle East

Although Christians are distinctly in the minority in most Middle Eastern countries, a few Christian sects, notably the Copts and the Maronites, play major roles in the culture of their nations. The group most familiar to Americans is the Maronite Christians of Lebanon, whose ranks include such familiar names as entertainers Danny Thomas, Paul Anka and Salma Hayek, author Kahlil Gibran, activist Ralph Nader and diplomat Philip Habib.

Iraq's Assyrians

Along with the Kurds and the Marsh Arabs, the Assyrian Christians are one of Iraq's largest minority groups. Some 1.3 million of them dwell there, mainly in Iraq's northern regions; they speak Aramaic and claim to be Iraq's founding people.

Egypt's Copts

The Copts, who practice an Orthodox form of Christianity, are plentiful in Egypt, numbering some 7 million and forming as much as 10% of the population. This single largest community of Christians in the Middle East practices one of the earliest forms of the religion.

Lebanon's Maronites

As many as 900,000 Maronites are believed to live in Lebanon, where they make up some 25% of the population. Although their rites are Orthodox, they are in communion with the Vatican. They are named for their first patriarch, John Maron, elected in A.D. 685.

The Saudis

KINGDOM OF SAUDI ARABIA

Population 27,019,731

Religion 100% Muslim, vast majority Sunni

Defining Moment The 1936 discovery of vast oil reserves catapulted the nation into modernity—and enormous wealth

WITHIN THE MUSLIM WORLD, Saudi Arabia is regarded with deep respect, for it is the birthplace of Muhammad; the cradle of Islam; and the site of Medina and Mecca, its most sacred cities. One of the five pillars of Islam is the injunction for each believer to make the pilgrimage, or *hajj*, to Mecca. Every year 2 million of the devout complete the journey; many of them add the honorific *hajji* to their name as a sign of their passage.

For long centuries, this land was distinguished primarily for its centrality to Islam, but the nation was put on a fast track to modernity when oil was discovered under its desert sands in 1936. The nation sits atop a mind-boggling 25% of the world's proven reserves of oil—and that accounts for the dynamic modern skyline of the capital city of Riyadh, right.

Oil brought Americans and Saudis together. Since the predecessor of today's Saudi Aramco oil company went into operation in 1933, a relationship based on mutual profit has kept the Saudis' face turned toward the West. Yet oil—and the perennially divisive question of Israel—has also driven the nations apart. When the U.S. bailed out a reeling Israel in the 1973 Yom Kippur War with a massive airlift of military matériel, the Saudis retaliated by turning off the oil spigot, plunging the U.S. into a lengthy economic downturn.

The oil alliance survived that rough patch, and for long years the Saudis have acted as a force for moderation in the Middle East, as in the 1991 Gulf War, when more than 300,000 U.S. and allied troops mustered in the Saudi desert before liberating Kuwait from Iraq's grasp.

OIL WEALTH ALSO BRED TERROR IN Saudi Arabia. Al-Qaeda kingpin Osama bin Laden is a member of a wealthy Saudi family, and 15 of the 19 hijackers in the 9/11 attacks on the U.S. were Saudis. Bin Laden's hatred of the U.S., his patron in his days as a *mujahid* in Afghanistan, is believed to date from the Gulf War, when the sight of U.S. soldiers based in Saudi Arabia—especially women driving jeeps with heads uncovered, wearing shorts—infuriated him. All U.S. troops departed the nation in 2003.

Muslim clerics play a strong role in setting Saudi cultural standards, and the nation has been rocked by the great religious revival that has reshaped the Muslim world in recent decades. The Saudis themselves have suffered at the hands of the jihadists: in addition to the more than 40 foreign nationals who have died in a string of attacks since 2003, four Saudi nationals died in the April 21, 2004, bombing of a Saudi security-forces building in Riyadh. ■

LOOKING UP: At 920 ft., Kingdom Centre in Riyadh, owned by a Saudi prince, is the largest building in Saudi Arabia. It opened in 2002

The House of Saud

Modern Saudi Arabia is the creation of the man whose name it bears: King Ibn Saud (1882-1953). An early proponent of Arab nationalism, he took control of Riyadh in 1901, when he was only 19, and in 1932 he merged the separate regions of Hejaz and Nejd to form the kingdom of Saudi Arabia; the third major region, Asir, joined the union the next year—just in time for the discovery of oil in 1936.

The extensive Saudi royal family still rules the kingdom. The current monarch, King Abdullah, right, served as regent after his half brother, King Fahd, was felled by a stroke in 1995; he took the title of King following Fahd's death in 2005.

LEONHARD GOEGER—REUTERS—CORBIS

GILLES BASSIGNAC—GAMMA

GILLES BASSIGNAC—BAMMA

Of Princes and Petrodollars

The transformation of Saudi Arabia by its vast resources of petroleum is a tale worthy of, well, *1001 Arabian Nights*. Once known for its wandering Bedouins and beckoning oases, the nation now is fabled for its extreme displays of wealth. A large workforce of 5 million foreign nationals does much of the nation's menial work, while upper-crust Saudis cruise the vast shopping mall at the base of Riyadh's Kingdom Centre, left. Above, Saudi businessmen examine a model of a city proposed for construction on an island in the Red Sea. Price tag: $26 billion.

Caught midway between the call of the muezzin and the lure of the credit card, Saudi Arabia is a bellwether nation in the Middle East; a swing either to the West or to Islamist militancy would reverberate throughout the world.

The Power of Wahhabism

Saudi Arabia is the home of Wahhabism, a reformist school of Islam founded by Muhammad ibn 'Abddul al-Wahhab in 1745. Not unlike the Protestant Reformation in Europe, whose goal was to purify Christianity and return it to first principles, Wahhabism caught fire with everyday Arabs, sweeping across the Arabian peninsula and uniting tribes under its banner.

King Ibn Saud, founder of the modern Saudi nation, was a descendant of Wahhabi leaders, and after he unified the kingdom in 1932, he returned the reformist school to a central place in its society. Today most Saudi children, below, are schooled in the fundamentalist form of Islam, considered one of the driving engines of modern militant Islamism.

FRANCO PAGETTI—POLARIS

The Egyptians

ARAB REPUBLIC OF EGYPT

Population 77,505,756

Religions Sunni Muslim, 94%; Copts, 5%

Defining Moment Anwar Sadat's decision to reach out to Israel has kept Egypt one of the most stable nations in the Middle East

SPRINGTIME IS A FESTIVE SEASON in Egypt, especially in Dahab, a laid-back Red Sea resort famous for its scuba divers and hippies. But terrorists broke up the party on April 24, 2006, setting off three explosions along Dahab's beachside promenade, killing 23 people, including four foreigners. Days later, two suicide bombers attacked an international peace-keeping base and an Egyptian police vehicle in the northern Sinai peninsula but killed only themselves.

The Dahab attacks were the third major strike on Egypt's Red Sea resorts in 18 months. They came as President Hosni Mubarak prepared to welcome political and business leaders to Egypt for a World Economic Forum gathering in May. The bombings underscored Mubarak's inability to eliminate the terrorist threat, which has hurt the country's $7 billion tourism industry.

Yet that is only one of the regime's problems. Long-simmering sectarian tensions erupted into rioting and street fighting between Muslim fundamentalists and Coptic Christians in Alexandria in mid-April. Only days later, Cairo police clashed with demonstrators protesting disciplinary action against two high-court judges, Mahmoud Mekki and Hisham Bastawisi. The pair had alleged widespread vote rigging in the November 2005 parliamentary elections and called for the independence of Egypt's judiciary—an embarrassing episode for a government that has been urged by the Bush Administration to implement democratic reform.

The next month was no better: on May 1, hundreds of marchers wound through the capital's traffic-gnarled streets pumping their fists and chanting, "O freedom, where are you, where are you? ... Mubarak stands between me and you!" The government had fully expected such a clash. More than 10,000 black-clad riot police had sealed off entire areas of the city in an attempt to prevent demonstrators from expressing their support for the judges.

TIME witnessed plainclothes thugs, who were apparently taking orders from police, attack the fleeing protesters with fists and truncheons. One woman was thrown to the ground, kicked and punched as she knelt on her hands and knees. At least six journalists were detained briefly, and several were beaten. Later in May, security officers seized hundreds more democracy advocates, including Internet bloggers; some were arrested, others roughed up and released.

SADLY, THESE SCENES WERE TAKING place in a nation that is considered a staunch friend and ally of the U.S.'s in the Middle East. In the 1950s, under the fiery Arab nationalist Gamal Abdel Nasser, Egypt had tangled with the U.S., and the two nations remained estranged during the Six-Day War and the Yom Kippur War. But after Anwar Sadat's turnaround on the subject of Israel led to the successful Camp David summit of 1978, and Egypt became the first Arab nation to recognize and make peace with Israel, the U.S. has regarded Egypt as a force for moderation in the region.

Mubarak has struggled with homegrown terrorists throughout his time in office. Sadat was murdered by rebel soldiers influenced by

PAST TENSE: Egypt's ancient monuments are world-known, but a terrorist attack that killed more than 60 people in 1997 has sent tourism into a tailspin

Islamic Jihad, the terrorist group later led by Ayman al-Zawahiri, al-Qaeda's No. 2 man in 2006. Sheik Omar Abdel Rahman, who was convicted in 1995 of planning a string of terrorist acts in the U.S., is another member of Islamic Jihad. The group also staged the 1997 massacre of more than 60 foreign tourists at Luxor.

MUBARAK, 78, WAS RE-ELECTED IN September 2005 on a platform of political and economic reform. As a close U.S. ally and one of its biggest recipients of military aid, he has lately had to walk a fine line, continuing to keep his tight rein on power while paying lip service to the kind of democratization that the Bush Administration hopes will spread in the Middle East.

Mubarak has argued that the mere fact that Egyptians are protesting is "evidence of democracy," but the scenes on Cairo's streets have left little doubt about the Mubarak regime's lack of tolerance for any real opposition. Mubarak's chief opponent in the 2005 election, Ayman Nour, was arrested three months after the vote and charged with election fraud. He is serving a five-year term in a Cairo jail. ■

Profiting from the Past

Egypt's history has a promising future. Since Britain's Howard Carter became the first man in centuries to enter the tomb of King Tutankhamen in 1923, the world's fascination with the hieroglyphs and mummies, pyramids and sphinxes of ancient Egypt has never declined. A new exhibit of treasures from Tut's tomb toured the U.S. in 2005 and 2006, drawing record crowds to many museums. Even more important, there may be discoveries yet to come.

In 2006, Zawi Hawass, the scholar-showman who is the head of Egypt's antiquities council, announced that a new tomb, the first untouched burial vault to be located since Carter's time, had been discovered in Egypt's Valley of the Kings. Although no mummies were found, the coffin was filled with ancient embalming materials, strips of linen and funerary garlands and collars made of dried flowers. But Egypt may not profit from the new findings until the world's tourists once again feel they will be safe during their visit.

Mubarak's Perspective, 2006

Egyptian President Hosni Mubarak leads one of the few Arab nations that has made peace with Israel. In the last weeks of July 2006, as Israel and Hizballah were battling in Lebanon, Mubarak offered written responses to questions submitted by TIME Cairo bureau chief Scott MacLeod concerning his view of the crisis. Excerpts:

TIME: How do you see Hizballah and Hamas?

MUBARAK: Both need to reassess their gains and losses. There are many lessons to learn from the current crises. I hope this gets through to their leaders for the sake of the Palestinian and Lebanese peoples. Hamas, all other Palestinian factions and [Palestinian President Mahmoud Abbas, also known as] Abu Mazen have to set aside their differences and speak in one voice. They have to prove that there exists a Palestinian partner able to negotiate a peace settlement with Israel. As to Hizballah, they are part and parcel of the Lebanese people's fabric. However, nobody should be allowed to establish a state within the state.

TIME: How do you see Israel's response?

MUBARAK: Disproportionate, to say the least. Israel's response demonstrated a collective punishment against the Palestinians and the Lebanese. The bloodshed and the destruction caused by the Israelis went way too far. This disproportionate response triggered an increasing rage within the Arabs, Muslims and worldwide. Hostage situations have to be tackled with a great deal of wisdom and caution.

TIME: How did the U.S. and the international community respond to the crisis?

MUBARAK: A bit too little, too late. The situation could have been contained at its early stage. Instead, it has been allowed to aggravate. An urgent and serious démarche [diplomatic maneuver] by the international community is most needed.

The Israelis

STATE OF ISRAEL

Population 6,276,883

Religions Jewish, 80%; Muslim, 18% (mainly Sunni); Christian 2%

Defining Moments The nation's founding and the Six-Day War left Israel in charge of large numbers of displaced Palestinians

WHAT IS ISRAEL? WHO ARE the Israelis? As the land promised to the Jews in the Old Testament approaches the 60th anniversary of its founding as a modern nation, Israelis are still struggling to define themselves.

Consider warfare. For Israel, it seems, winning wars can be almost as hazardous as losing them. The Six-Day War of 1967 marked Israel's passage into national adulthood in ways both triumphal and tragic. In a stroke, Israelis nearly tripled the size of their territory, but they also became the unwilling custodians of millions of Arab lives in the West Bank and Gaza.

After the war, the nation's founding Prime Minister, David Ben-Gurion warned Israel that it should give back all the captured territories quickly, "for holding on to them would distort, and might ultimately destroy, the Jewish state." In 1967, PM Levi Eshkol offered to return almost all the territories to the Arabs in exchange for recognition and a promise to negotiate peace. Arab states responded thunderously with their famous "three nos"—no recognition of Israel, no negotiation, no peace. Thus began, almost as an afterthought, decades of occupation that have taught Israel painful lessons: conquest is easier than control, and the transition from David to Goliath is a difficult one.

FOR DECADES, ISRAELIS HAVE FOUGHT additional wars with their neighbors and quelled repeated uprisings from Arabs within its borders, but have still moved fitfully toward peace— even as they created a thriving modern civilization in the desert. Israel gave back the Sinai Peninsula to Egypt after the 1978 Camp David Accords. It exchanged mutual recognition with the Palestine Liberation Organization in 1993, normalized relations with Jordan in 1994 and gave up control of Gaza in 2005.

This balancing act—fighting when necessary (and sometimes when it wasn't), negotiating when possible (and occasionally when it didn't seem to be)—speaks eloquently of the country's contradictions. Israel, Saul Bellow wrote in his 1975 book, *To Jerusalem and Back,* "is both a garrison state and a cultivated society, both Spartan and Athenian." Most Israelis ache for their nation to be less of the former and more of the latter, but trumping that dream is a more elemental goal: to survive.

ISRAEL'S NATIONAL PREDICAMENT IS this: if an overwhelming superiority of arms could settle the Palestinian question, Israel would have achieved a lasting peace decades ago. But history has shown it cannot, and generations of Israelis have been trapped in that chasm. They have tried to impose a military solution on the political problem of the Palestinian desire for a homeland while they have sought a political solution to the military problem of the continuing desire of some Palestinian militants to drive all Jews into the sea.

A more recent problem is the concern that increasing populations of Palestinians in the occupied territories might lead to the Jews' becoming a demographic minority within Israel. So leaders from Yitzhak Rabin to Ariel Sharon crowded the decade

since 1993's Oslo Accords with more overtures toward peace—or at least disentanglement—than were seen in the previous 25 years. In 1995, PM Benjamin Netanyahu signed the Wye River Memorandum, giving the Palestinian Authority greater control in Gaza and the West Bank. In 2000, Ehud Barak implemented a unilateral withdrawal from the "security zone" that Israeli troops had occupied in southern Lebanon for almost 20 years. In 2002, Sharon ordered the construction of a 415-mile-long defensive barrier that would partition the West Bank from Israel. Three years later, Sharon decided, in effect, to hand Gaza back to the Palestinians, without negotiations.

IN THE SUMMER OF 2006, HOWEVER, the policy of disengagement was upended when new PM Ehud Olmert traded the carrot for the stick, sending troops and tanks rolling into Lebanon and laying waste to Beirut after Hizballah militants captured two Israeli soldiers. As this book goes to press, the aftershocks of Israel's tough new line were just starting to register. But there is little doubt that Israel's future was foretold by elder statesman Chaim Weizmann in 1949, when the nation was only a year old. "I am certain," he wrote, "that the world will judge the Jewish state by what it will do with the Arabs." ∎

Prime Ministers of Israel, 1948–2006

David Ben-Gurion	1948–53
Moshe Sharett	1953–55
David Ben-Gurion	1955–63
Levi Eshkol	1963–69
Yigal Allon	1969
Golda Meir	1969–74
Yitzhak Rabin	1974–77
Menachem Begin	1977–83
Yitzhak Shamir	1983–84
Shimon Peres	1984–86
Yitzhak Shamir	1986–92
Yitzhak Rabin	1992–95
Shimon Peres	1995–96
Benjamin Netanyahu	1996–99
Ehud Barak	1999–2001
Ariel Sharon	2001–06
Ehud Olmert	2006

KEEP OUT: Acknowledging it is a garrison state, Israel has begun building security barriers to seal its borders. This wall is in the West Bank

Theodor Herzl and Zionism

Although he did not invent Zionism, which takes its name from the ancient Hebrew word for a mountain near Jerusalem, Theodor Herzl is considered the father of the movement that eventually led to the founding of a Jewish state. No stranger to anti-Semitism in his native Austria-Hungary, he was shocked to find it flourishing in Paris when he moved there as a journalist in 1891. Herzl's belief that Jews must organize and emigrate to a homeland where "the offensive cry of 'Jew' may become an honorable appellation like German, Englishman, Frenchman" displeased assimilationist Jews. But it resonated with nationalistic Jews. Herzl organized a world congress in 1897 and later wrote in his diary that this conference had "founded the Jewish state. If I said this aloud today, I would be greeted by universal laughter. Perhaps in five years, and certainly in fifty, everyone will agree." Forty-nine years after the conference ended, Israel was born.

The Palestinians

PALESTINIAN AUTHORITY TERRITORIES

Population West Bank, 2.4 million;
Gaza Strip, 1.4 million

Religion Sunni Muslim, 90%

Defining Moment After the Oslo Accords of
1993, the Palestinian Authority took control
of daily life in the West Bank and Gaza Strip

NOTHING RANKLES PALESTINIANS more than the argument that before the 1948 founding of Israel, Palestine was "a land without a people," waiting to be settled by the Jews, "a people without a land." In truth, Palestinians have inhabited the land "from the river to the sea" (a popular Arabic reference to the territory between the Jordan River and the Mediterranean Sea) almost from the time that Jews first settled there in the days of the Bible.

How ancient are these competing claims to the same land? Here's one clue: the Palestinian name for their homeland is Falastin (the consonant sound *p* doesn't occur in most Arabic dialects): the term is derived from the ancient Philistines, whose giant Goliath did battle with the Jewish David in the Old Testament.

On the other side of the fence, Israelis find few historical claims more galling than the idea that a long-standing tradition of Palestinian independence was crushed by the Zionists in 1948. In truth, Palestine was never an independent nation; it has always been a province or colony of faraway empires like Babylon, Rome, the Ottomans—or of powerful local sheikdoms. The British protectorate of Palestine was a colonial contrivance created by the League of Nations after World War I.

HERE'S SOMETHING BOTH SIDES CAN agree on: nothing has done more to forge a Palestinian identity and foster a longing for independence than dispossession. Since 1948, generations of Palestinians have cultivated an idealized vision of their shared past. The loss of village life's quiet joys amid the olive groves haunts the dreams of many Palestinians who were born in refugee camps decades after al-Nakbar—Arabic for "the Catastrophe," the term by which Palestinians refer to Israel's founding.

The "right of return"—a demand that the descendants of all Palestinians sent into exile by the 1948 war be allowed to reclaim their lost property—has become one of the chief obstacles to a comprehensive peace. Israeli officials fear that allowing more than 1 million Palestinians to move into Israel and take over homes would threaten their country's security and its Jewish identity.

TIME OFF: Palestinian residents of the Gaza Strip enjoy the Mediterranean

THERE IS LITTLE DISAGREEMENT among states in the region about what an ideal peace between Israel and the Palestinians would involve. Since before World War II, most reasonable observers have known that sooner or later, two states—one with a Jewish majority, one with an Arab one—would share the land "from the river to the sea." That was the basis of the 2000 talks between Israel and the Palestinians at Camp David; it was acknowledged at the meeting of Arab states in Beirut in 2002, when they committed to "normal relations" with Israel if it withdrew to its pre-1967 borders; it was the basis of the road map adopted by the U.S. and other powers in 2003; and it was accepted, finally, by Israel's old hawk Ariel Sharon, although he adopted a policy of unilateral "disengagement" from the Palestinians.

"We know we can't wind this up with guns and tanks," Israel's Deputy Prime Minister, Shimon Peres, told TIME in 2006. "The final solution has to be done diplomatically." ∎

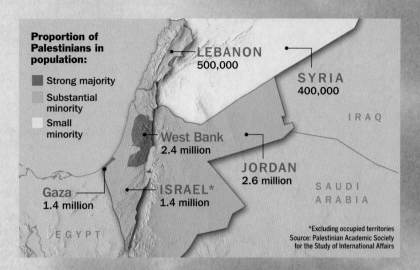

Proportion of Palestinians in population:

- ■ Strong majority
- ■ Substantial minority
- □ Small minority

LEBANON 500,000

SYRIA 400,000

IRAQ

West Bank 2.4 million

JORDAN 2.6 million

SAUDI ARABIA

Gaza 1.4 million

ISRAEL* 1.4 million

EGYPT

*Excluding occupied territories
Source: Palestinian Academic Society for the Study of International Affairs

Mahmoud Abbas: Highwire Act

Palestinian Authority President Mahmoud Abbas, 71, hoped to preside over a new era of reconciliation with Israel. But his plans were thwarted when the militant Hamas party won the Palestinian elections in January 2006. Since Hamas has refused to renounce violence and recognize Israel's right to exist, the U.S., European Union and Israel cut off the flow of funds to the Palestinian Authority promised in the Oslo Accords of 1993, sending the West Bank and Gaza Strip economies reeling. The following September Abbas thought he had managed to succeed in convincing Hamas to roll back that position, but the group declared that it might accept a cease-fire with Israel, but would never recognize it. Back to the drawing board.

In the West Bank and Gaza, a Daily Struggle

For people who live as refugees, the scattering is not only physical but also cultural, economic and psychological. Since 1948, many Palestinians have embraced new lives and new lands; others have continued to live as exiles. In Jordan, where Palestinian expatriates dominate the economy and are thought to number half of the population, the quality of life is usually both predictable and bearable. Within Arab villages and refugee camps on the occupied West Bank and in the now semiautonomous Gaza Strip, life is neither. There, the economy consists almost entirely of providing menial, low-wage services to Israel, but it reflects the daily state of tension and the border closings that Israel imposes after terrorist attacks. Right, a woman takes a shortcut over Israel's security fence to her job.

When the border is closed, thousands of Palestinians are cut off from paychecks, and the economy reverts to barter, credit and welfare. Much of the last comes from groups like Hamas, which is widely viewed in the West as a terrorist organization but is seen by Palestinians primarily as a provider of education and health care and the guarantor of a social safety net that includes financial assistance during lean times.

BEFORE AND AFTER: On this page, smart cafés in Beirut's Hamra district in 2000; opposite, the devastated Haret Hreik neighborhood in Beirut, a Hizballah stronghold, on July 20, 2006

The Lebanese

REPUBLIC OF LEBANON

Population 3,826,018

Religions Muslim, 70%; Christian, 30%

Defining Moment Lebanon won its independence from France in 1944 but has never escaped Syria's domination

PERHAPS IT'S A MATTER OF DES-tiny: today's Lebanese are the descendants of Phoenician sea traders, the great merchant capitalists of the ancient world. Or perhaps it's a matter of geography: Lebanon's sun-soaked Mediter-ranean coast is a magnet for the jet-set. Whatever the reason, modern Lebanon is one of the most Western-ized of Middle Eastern nations, the place where the world's wealthy con-gregate to enjoy life in the bustling shops, cafés and restaurants of Beirut, the Paris of the Middle East.

That's the story suggested by the picture above—and it was accurate up until July 2006, when Lebanon found itself once again transformed into a killing ground for determined antagonists, who were prepared to turn it into a wasteland to achieve

their larger ends. The story of that Lebanon is told in the picture at top right of a devastated Beirut suburb.

HOW DID IT COME TO THIS? LIKE SO many other woes in the Middle East, Lebanon's misery began with its creation after World War I, when French colonial administrators separated the nation known as Syria under the Ottoman Empire into two parts. The first was the new, smaller Syria, a largely Sunni nation; the second was Lebanon, a polyglot state composed of Maronite Christians; the Druze, whose faith is a blend of Islam and Gnosticism; and both Sunni and Shi'ite Muslims. It was a formula for woe.

Syria never seemed to get the memo that Lebanon was a separate nation; it has dominated its younger sibling's politics for decades. When fighting between Christians and Muslims turned into a civil war in 1975, Syrian troops entered the country to "keep peace"; a few years later, Israeli forces moved in, chasing Palestinian guerrillas who had been staging raids from Lebanon on Israeli settlers.

The pattern was set: civil strife in Lebanon, plus harassment of Israelis by militias based there, kept the nation deeply unsettled roughly from 1975 to 1990. During that peri-od, Christian Phalangist militiamen massacred civilians during an Israeli occupation in 1982; 241 American and 58 French paratroopers were killed by suicide bombers from the militant group Hizballah in 1983; and the nation became a wasteland.

It wasn't until 1990 that peace finally came to Lebanon, thanks to a pact that put Syria in charge of Lebanon's foreign relations. In the years that followed, Beirut rebuilt itself into a new metropolis, gleam-ing and chic, once again the Middle East's City of Light. But it paid a price: Syria continued to dominate the nation's politics, its troops on the ground sending the message that Lebanon's elected government didn't run the country—Damascus did.

Syria proved its point when it demanded that its ally, Lebanese President Emile Lahoud, remain in office past the conclusion of his man-dated single six-year term. When Lebanon's parliament agreed, Rafik

Hariri, the billionaire Prime Minister who had shepherded the rebuilding of the nation, resigned. A few months later, he was murdered in a car bombing that claimed the lives of 16 others. Few doubted that Syria was behind the atrocity.

The murder shook Lebanon, and released several decades' worth of anti-Syrian feeling. Anti- and pro-Syrian forces scrambled to marshal supporters in giant, competing rallies in Beirut, sparking hopes of a "Cedar Revolution." And Syria seemed to relax its grip at last: in late April 2005, the last Syrian soldier left Lebanon.

Yet Prime Minister Fouad Siniora, appointed by Lahoud in 2005, presides over a weak government, and Lebanon's fate remains defined by larger players in the region. In July 2006 a new crisis erupted. When Hizballah militiamen took two Israelis hostage, the old pattern resumed: Israeli troops and tanks rolled in; Hizballah fighters dug into their sturdy bunkers and fired back; Hizballah's paymasters in Syria and Iran footed the bill. And once again, darkness fell on the people of Lebanon and the City of Light. ■

TOP: ERICH LESSING—ART RESOURCE, NY; BOTTOM: BETTMANN CORBIS.

Trading Masters of Ancient Oceans

Smaller than the state of Connecticut, Lebanon looms large in history. From the shores of Cana, Lebanon's name in biblical times, Phoenician galleys, left, their masts made from Lebanon's famed cedars, traversed the Mediterranean in the ancient world, embarking from such fabled ports as Tyre and Tripoli.

The high point of Phoenicia's trading empire, which was based on a league of independent ports that operated much like Greek city-states, dates from 1200–800 B.C.

A U.S. Landing in Lebanon, 1958

Americans are all too familiar with the fate of the U.S. Marines who were stationed in a barracks near the Beirut airport in 1983, serving as part of an international peacekeeping force: 241 of them were murdered by Hizballah suicide bombers. But an earlier U.S. mission to Lebanon is not so well remembered. In 1958 the government of Lebanon's Maronite President, the pro-West Camille Chamoun, was under assault from militant Islamic militias. At Chamoun's request, President Dwight D. Eisenhower sent a contingent of U.S. Marines to Lebanon. Their landing on July 15, 1958, above, may have resembled D-day, but it went unopposed, and the Marines came home three months later.

The Syrians

SYRIAN ARAB REPUBLIC

Population 18,488,752

Religions Sunni Muslim, 74%; Druze and other Islamic sects, 16%

Defining Moment After their unusual alliance during the first Gulf War, Syria and the U.S. have frequently been at odds

HOW DO THEY HATE THE WEST? Let us count the ways. During an anti-American rally in Damascus in 2000, the security forces controlled by Syrian President Bashar Ashad looked the other way as a mob stormed the grounds and ransacked the U.S. mission. Amid the 2005 protests over Danish cartoons viewed as mocking the Prophet Muhammad, demonstrators burned the Danish and Norwegian embassies in Damascus.

Although Syria joined the U.S.-led alliance that rolled back Saddam Hussein's takeover of Kuwait in 1993, relations between the two have been tense for years, as Syria, under both current President Bashar Assad and his father Hafez Assad, has played paymaster to worldwide terrorist groups. Bashar Assad has been outspoken in his support of Islamic militant groups like Hizballah in Lebanon and the Palestinian factions Hamas and Islamic Jihad.

U.S. officials believe that the Assad regime has secretly aided the ongoing Sunni insurgency in Iraq, providing passage for jihad volunteers and funds and safe haven for insurgency

leaders. At the start of the war in 2003, Arab jihadists who poured into Damascus en route to Baghdad were allowed to openly line up outside the Iraqi embassy just down the road from the U.S. embassy. At the time, the Bush Administration described Syria as a rogue nation and accused it of harboring chemical weapons. Two years later, the U.S. recalled its ambassador in Damascus after Syria, despite its denials, was strongly implicated in the 2005 assassination of former Lebanese Prime Minister Rafik Hariri.

SYRIA'S HATRED FOR ALL THINGS American seemed to have reached a peak on Sept. 12, 2006—note the date—when four Islamic militants shouting Muslim slogans staged an attack on the U.S. embassy in the heart of Damascus' diplomatic quarter, not far from Assad's own residence—in short, one of the most heavily protected neighborhoods in Syria, if not the Middle East. The attackers failed to kill any U.S. diplomats, and Syrian security guards managed to slay three of them.

Yet the Syrian regime itself may have more to worry about from this particular attack than the U.S. That's because the raid was not only an assault on the U.S. but also a bold challenge to Assad's rule. He knows that allowing terrorists to hit the embassy could be a casus belli for a U.S. military strike on Syria. Allowing mobs to chant slogans against the

U.S. is one thing, but internal terrorism tells the Syrian people something no dictator wishes to show: that the regime does not have as tight a grip on the country as it would like its citizens to believe.

In the complex politics of the Middle East, one can be a major funder of terrorism and a supporter of some militant groups yet be deeply at odds with others. The attack suggested that the Syrian regime's own long war with Islamic extremists may be heating up again. In 1982, the regime of Hafez Assad obliterated sections of the Syrian city of Hama, killing an estimated 20,000 people, to quell an uprising by the fundamentalist Muslim Brotherhood.

The Assad dynasty's iron rule has kept the lid on discontent for most of the time since. But during the past few years, new attacks seem to herald the return of violent extremists. In June 2006, four gunmen were killed trying to attack the building housing Syrian state television in one of the most prominent public squares in Damascus.

ASSAD, WHOSE REGIME IS OFFICIALLY secular despite its close alliance with the Islamic Republic of Iran, often casts himself as the champion of radical Islamic movements. In August 2006, in a speech openly ridiculing moderate Arab leaders, he hailed Hizballah's war in Lebanon as a stinging defeat for Israel that undercut U.S. plans for the region. But it is beginning to look as though at least some of the Islamists consider his regime the enemy too. In Syria's neck of the woods, there never seems to be a shortage of enemies—or a shortfall in ways to hate them. ∎

BELOW: SHAWN BALDWIN—CORBIS; RIGHT: ROGJT' HENRI BUREAU—SYGMA—CORBIS

THE LEADER: A poster of President Bashar Assad greets visitors to Qerdaha, the hometown of the dynasty that has ruled Syria since 1970

تقدمة الدكتورفوازا

Like Father, Like Son

For three decades, from 1970 to 2000, Hafez Assad, right, ruled Syria—and confounded the world. Six American Presidents found him frustrating, remote. The Egyptian pyramids lay to the southwest, but it was Assad who was dubbed the Sphinx. Austere, he neither smoked nor drank. The onetime fighter-jet pilot who led a 1970 military coup—or, as he dubbed it, a "corrective movement"—was legendary for his marathon negotiating sessions and infuriating intransigence. Although in 1973 he sent hundreds of tanks swarming toward Israel on the Day of Atonement in a concerted effort with Egypt to regain Arab territory, once he'd lost the Yom Kippur War, he kept to the truce with utmost scrupulousness. On his watch, Syria was a stalwart of the State Department's terrorism list since its inception in 1979—but it was also part of the anti-Iraq coalition that fought in the Gulf War.

When Bashar Assad, trained as an ophthalmologist, came to power after his father's death, there was much conjecture that he would, well, cast a different eye on Syria's role in the world and its relationship with the West. But after a brief "Damascus Spring" when personal liberties were enlarged, Bashar embraced the ways of his father, ruling Syria with an iron fist.

The Jordanians

THE HASHEMITE KINGDOM OF JORDAN

Population 5,611,202

Religions Sunni Muslim 92%; Christian 6%

Defining Moment Jordan lost possession of the sacred sites of East Jerusalem to Israel in the Six-Day War of 1967

HISTORY FLOWS THROUGH JORdan like the river from which the country takes its name—from the site where many scholars believe Jesus was baptized by John to the mountain from which Moses peered into the promised land, where he would never set foot. Centuries later, it was in Jordan that T.E. Lawrence ("Lawrence of Arabia") raised an army of Bedouins and staged raids on the east flank of the Ottoman Empire during World War I. Lawrence called Jordan a "vast, echoing and Godlike" place where even the proudest of men gazed into the night sky and were "shamed into pettiness by the innumerable silences of stars."

Lawrence's machinations in the desert contributed to the country's founding. Part of a League of Na-

tions mandate entrusted to Britain after the war, the Emirate of Transjordan was born in 1921 when London's colonial authorities bisected the Mandate along the Jordan River (the territory to the west became Israel and Palestine) and installed King Abdullah I on the throne. Granted independence in 1946, Jordan was buffeted by the exodus of Palestinian refugees two years later, when the state of Israel was born, and its fragile stability was rocked in 1951, when Abdullah was assassinated by a Palestinian militant acting on rumors that the King was contemplating peace negotiations with Israel. At Abdullah's side when he was killed was Hussein, the grandson who would succeed him.

HUSSEIN REIGNED FROM 1952 UNTIL his death in 1999. Ruling the poor stepson of the Arab world (Jordan lacks the oil wealth of Saudi Arabia, the vast territory of Iraq or the military might of Syria), Hussein strove to maintain a delicate balance between Arab nationalism and accommodation with Western patrons like

the U.S., whose aid was essential.

Along the way, Jordan was rocked by upheavals. In 1967 it lost all of its territory west of the Jordan river (the West Bank) and the Old City of Jerusalem to Israel, when King Hussein followed Egypt's Gamal Abdel Nasser into the war. In 1970's Black September crisis, Palestinian militants tried to topple Hussein's government, leading to their expulsion. In 2005 Jordan paid a steep price for its friendships in the West, as bombers from al-Qaeda in Iraq blew up three hotels in the capital city of Amman, killing 60 people.

Through it all, Jordan has seldom strayed from the path of moderation. In 1994, it became only the second Arab country (after Egypt) to sign a peace treaty with Israel, and under U.S.-educated King Abdullah II, it remains a model of tolerance in the Middle East: women in Western-style dress can be seen on the streets, alcohol is served in the restaurants, and Americans are thanked for being the countrymen of the respected Queen Noor. ∎

GLOAMING: Yes, there are more rivers in Jordan than the familiar

A Heritage in Natural Stone

Familiar to Americans after it was used as the unforgettable setting for the conclusion of the movie *Indiana Jones and the Last Crusade,* the treasury at Petra is one of the most dazzling archaeological sites in the world. It was carved by the Nabataeans, a tribe of Semitic nomads, into the red cliff face of a remote sandstone canyon sometime around 400 B.C., although the precise date in uncertain.

Straddling a vital point on the overland trade routes between the Mediterranean and the Far East, the city of Petra prospered for centuries, until being undone by natural and financial disasters. The former took the form of an earthquake, which devastated the

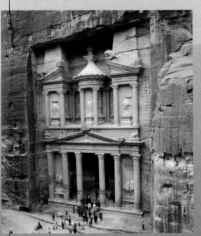

citadel's elaborate systems of wells, dams and cisterns. The latter came in the guise of new technology: starting in the 2nd century A.D., traders from the Orient began sailing across the Indian Ocean and up the Red Sea, making the overland route obsolete.

Deprived of steady supplies of both water and money, Petra quickly turned into a ghost town. For more than 1,500 years, it was abandoned and forgotten. Then, in 1812, Johann Ludwig Burckhardt, a Swiss explorer who spoke fluent Arabic, disguised himself as a local tribesman and bribed desert guides to show him the lost city that was rumored to lie hidden in the Jordanian sands. Indiana Jones would have liked that story.

Jordan's American Queen

I want to see your father," the 42-year-old King Hussein told the 26-year-old American, Lisa Halaby, in 1978. Although their friendship up to that point had been strictly professional (she was working on an urban planning project in Jordan), the recent Princeton graduate suspected, correctly, that Hussein intended to propose. Thus did Halaby, whose father was Najeeb Halaby, a former CEO of Pan-American World Airways, become Queen Noor. Converting to Islam shortly before her marriage, she took as her royal name the Arabic word meaning "light," beginning a 22-year partnership, chronicled in her 2003 memoir, *Leap of Faith,* that captivated the public in both her native and adopted countries.

Al-Qaeda's Terror Strike in Jordan

The backyard camp for the Crusader army is now in the range of fire of the holy warriors," said a statement issued by al-Qaeda in Iraq hours after bombs exploded simultaneously at three hotels in Amman, Jordan on Nov. 9, 2005, killing 60 people and wounding hundreds. (Because Jordanian notation places the number of the day first, followed by the month, the date is remembered in Jordan as 9/11.) An Iraqi woman who was later captured confessed that she was intended to be the bomber of a fourth hotel, but her explosive belt failed to detonate.

The bombings—whose precision timing is a hallmark of al-Qaeda—turned out to be the work of Jordanian native and al-Qaeda in Iraq leader Abu Mousab al-Zarqawi. They pushed Amman's security apparatus into overdrive, as Jordanian agents began gathering information about al-Zarqawi and his supporters throughout the Arab world. It is unknown whether intelligence supplied by Jordan played any role in the U.S. aerial bombardment that killed al-Zarqawi in June 2006.

The Iraqis

REPUBLIC OF IRAQ

Population 25,374,691

Religions Shi'ite:,60% to 65%; Sunni, 32% to 37%; Christian , 3%

Defining Moment Saddam Hussein lost Kuwait—but stayed in power—in 1991

LIKE MANY OF THE MODERN states of the Middle East, Iraq existed on no map and in no one's mind before it was cobbled into existence by British colonial overseers after World War I. Having anointed King Abdullah as Jordan's King, London chose his brother Faisal to reign over its neighbor to the east, Iraq, in 1921. (The brothers came from a Hashemite family: they could trace their lineage back to relatives of the Prophet Muhammad.) In Iraq's case, the arbitrary designation of national frontiers by Europeans would prove highly clumsy:

the new country forced together a combustible mix of mutually antagonistic factions, Shi'ites, Sunnis and Kurds, each of which regarded itself as a separate nation deserving its own homeland.

Adding to Iraq's volatility was an ancient claim by tribal chiefs in Baghdad to rule over the area now known as Kuwait, which British authorities partitioned into a separate country after World War I. (Similarly, Persia's leaders for a thousand years felt possessive about vast swaths of Iraqi territory.) Granted independence in 1932, Iraq was quickly plunged into religious and ethnic turmoil. That situation was aggravated by the rising importance of oil, discovered in Iraq in 1927, which created a new middle class—secular, urban, educated—that had little love for Britain's influence in the country but also felt little kinship for the staunchly traditional tribes of the countryside.

AFTER 1948, THE ONE SUBJECT ON which all Iraqis seemed to agree was hatred of Israel, but Iraq's actions in the 1948 war against the new Jewish

state backfired when a pipeline running through Israel was severed, cutting Iraq's oil revenue in half.

A decade later, rising popular discontent was exploited by a group of army officers who overthrew the monarchy, executed the King, along with many members of his family, and proclaimed Iraq a republic. A series of bloody coups and counter-coups (along with Kurdish rebellions and a 1961 landing by British troops to stop Iraqi from seizing Kuwait) kept the country teetering on the brink of anarchy through the 1960s.

Life improved for Iraqis in the 1970s: although border disputes continued with Kuwait and Iran, oil revenue made the country prosperous and powerful. Internal tensions—indeed, all dispute or dissent of any kind—were muffled by the bloody repression by the Baath Party regime that took power in a 1968 coup, under the leadership of general (later President) Ahmed Hassan al-Bakr.

In 1979, the aging al-Bakr was eased aside by his chosen successor, Saddam Hussein. Within months, Iraq's brief period of relative stability was the stuff of history. ∎

ROUTINE : This April 2004 car bombing in al-Ramadi—and many others that preceded and followed it around the nation—made violence and chaos all too familiar in Iraq

Of Babel and the Bible

Ancient Mesopotamia, most of which was located in the land we now call Iraq, is often called the cradle of civilization. Records dating back more than 40 centuries describe the glories of a society that pioneered agriculture, gave us some of the first written laws and conquered the known world. Many scholars believe that the ziggurats erected by the Mesopotamians to facilitate contact with their gods were the inspiration for the biblical story of the Tower of Babel, left.

Indeed, the name "Babel" may come from the city of Babylon, which was located in the south of what is now Iraq and was one of the leading cultural centers of the Mesopotamian Empire. And scientists are still searching, using cameras on satellites high above the planet, for the site of the Garden of Eden, which the Old Testament says was located between the Tigris and Euphrates rivers, which run through modern Iraq.

Three Years ... and Counting ... in an Uncivil War

Secretary of Defense Donald Rumsfeld predicted in October 2003, five months after the U.S. and its allies took down Saddam Hussein's regime in Iraq, that the occupation of the nation would be "a long, hard slog." Almost three years later, in September 2006, his analysis still rang true: some 135,000 U.S. troops were on duty in Iraq, joined by 7,200 British troops and a sprinkling of soldiers from other allies.

TIME correspondent Aparisim Ghosh reported a sign of progress in the magazine's Aug. 14, 2006, issue. The road leading from the Baghdad airport into the city, long known as the Highway of Death, had become less deadly in recent months; attacks that used to occur daily had given way to occasional strikes, such as the twin suicide bombings in May that killed 14 Iraqis. But insurgent activity in Iraq, once directed mainly at U.S. soldiers, increasingly seemed to be a sectarian matter between

Sunnis and Shi'ites. As reported by Ghosh: "American officials and Iraqi politicians who live and work in the fortified bubble of the Green Zone [headquarters of the U.S. occupation in Baghdad] are still reluctant to use the words civil war. At the start of this year, they were dismissing an all-out battle between sects as impossible. In March they were saying it was improbable. Now they cautiously suggest it is not inevitable." Another sign of the times: when asked in March 2006 when the U.S. might begin withdrawing its troops from Iraq, President George W. Bush, who will step down in January 2009, said, "That will be decided by future presidents."

اسرائیل باید از صفحه روزگار محو شود

ISREAL MUST BE WIPED OUT THE WORLD

The Iranians

ISLAMIC REPUBLIC OF IRAN

Population 67,503,205

Religions Shi'ite 89%; Sunni 9%; other 2%

Defining Moment The 1979 revolution turned Iran from a pro-West nation into a militantly Islamist, mullah-dominated state

LIKE TURKEY, IRAN LIES AT THE crossroads of Europe and Asia, and like the Turks, Iranians are a distinct ethnic group in the Middle East: they are Persians, not Arabs, and their native tongue is Farsi, not Arabic. Iran has been deeply Muslim since the 7th century A.D., and most Iranians are Shi'ites. For centuries Iran was the only Islamic nation not under Sunni control.

The 1979 revolution led by Ayatullah Khomeini turned Iran into a fundamentalist theocracy. After a period of relative moderation under President Mohammed Khatami, Iran's mullahs are once again riding high since tough-talking Mahmoud Ahmadinejad was elected President in 2005. Under the former mayor of Tehran, Iran has been flexing its muscles on the world stage. With its economy pumped up by oil wealth, Ahmadinejad's Iran perceives itself as a growing power in world affairs, one that deserves respect—and the right to develop nuclear power.

As of the fall of 2006, things were going Iran's way in the Middle East. The U.S. occupation helped give the long-repressed Shi'ite minority much more power in Iraq, and new Prime Minister Nouri al-Maliki paid his respects in a state visit to Iran in September. In Lebanon, Iran's long support of Hizballah paid off when the militant group survived a tough Israeli onslaught in the summer.

Yet if militant Islamists control Iran's government, it is actually a deeply divided nation, with a large population of disaffected, Western-leaning young people. When Ahmadinejad declared he would donate millions to help Hizballah rebuild Lebanon after the 2006 conflict with Israel, TIME's Azadeh Moaveni reported that the spending on a faraway Arab community infuriated many Iranians and revived an ugly Persian chauvinism that considers Arabs uncultured and backward.

The biggest task confronting Iran's leader may involve butter, rather than guns (and nukes): despite the oil boom, in September 2006, the rate of inflation was at least 19%, and unemployment was up to 15%. ■

REMEMBERING: More than 10,000 Iranians marched through Tehran on Nov. 2, 2005, to celebrate the anniversary of the taking of U.S. hostages in 1979

Iran's Nuclear Dreams

Throughout 2005 and 2006, Iran's President, Mahmoud Ahmadinejad, was at loggerheads with the U.S. and other Western nations over the question of nuclear power: he insisted his nation had the right to enrich uranium for peaceful use (above, Iran's plant outside Isfahan in 2005). The U.S. and several European allies were unconvinced; they passed a resolution in the U.N. Security Council demanding that Iran cease enriching uranium by Aug. 31, 2006. When Iran failed to heed the deadline, the U.S. began lobbying for sanctions, but some analysts thought Iran might agree to a temporary suspension of development in return for comprehensive talks about its nuclear future. The issue is one of the most pressing in today's Middle East.

The Glory of Persia

Persia is one of humanity's oldest, grandest civilizations; under early leaders Cyrus the Great and Darius I, left, the Persian (or Achaemenid) Empire grew to girdle the Middle East, reaching from India to Egypt around 500 B.C. After Alexander the Great conquered Persia and burned the capital city of Persepolis, below, in 330 B.C., Persians were more often subjects than rulers, at various times owing fealty to the Seleucids, the Parthians and the Sasanians.

Islam came to Persia soon after Muhammad's death, when Arab Muslims conquered the nation in A.D. 641, and it flourished with arts and sciences in the glorious first centuries of Islam. Mongols invaded Persia in the 13th century, leaving behind a shaken civilization. From the ruins a fundamentalist form of Islam, the Safaviyeh Order, grew in power, gradually taking control of the nation in a political and cultural revolution that foreshadowed the Islamist movement that would bring Ayatullah Khomeini into power 700 years later.

Under the Safavid dynasty, Persia became a militantly Shi'ite nation, an identity it still retains. Sunnis were persecuted and the nation was run as a theocracy, although the Safavid Shahs also encouraged the arts and crafts, leading to a renaissance in the visual arts that produced exquisite Persian carpets, mosques and paintings. Iran's famed Peacock Throne, below, is modeled on one commissioned by India's Mughal ruler Shah Jahan, builder of the Taj Mahal, which was brought to Persia in 1739 after Nader Shah invaded India and defeated the Mughals.

In recent centuries Persians fought to retain their identity as Western powers began to eye the region. An internal revolution kept the hereditary Shah in power but gave the nation its first constitution and parliament in 1906. Later in the 20th century, Iran (the nation's formal name since 1935) was often under the thumb of outside powers, until the 1979 revolution once again put the nation under the sway of fundamentalist clerics.

The Kurds

EXILES FEED ON HOPE," AESCHYLUS once wrote; if so, the Kurds have supped their fill in modern times. Although their numbers are large—at more than 30 million people, they outnumber the population of Saudi Arabia—the Kurdish people are the largest ethnic group in the world without a homeland of their own. Instead, in the evocative African term, they are "scatterlings," spread across remote stretches of Turkey, Iran, Syria and Iraq; collectively, these regions are called Kurdistan.

Ethnically distinct, Kurds are neither Turks nor Arabs nor Persians, although they live among all these peoples, and their language is related to but distinct from Persian (Farsi). Most Kurds are Sunni Muslims, though Iran's Kurds are more likely to be Shi'ites. They practice a moderate form of Islam: most women do not cover their heads or wear the chador. A small number of Kurds follow Judaism.

SALADIN, THE LEGENDARY ISLAMIC warrior and King who fought the Crusaders in the 12 century, was a Kurd, and modern-day Kurds like to believe they share his valor and ferocity. Denied a homeland by European powers after World War I, the Kurds, eternal outsiders, have tried to bargain, battle or simply will a Kurdish state into being, and they've occasionally achieved brief success.

A Kingdom of Kurdistan was proclaimed in northern Iraq in 1922 and lasted for two years before it was overrun by British and Iraqi troops. Another country with the same name in eastern Turkey lasted for two months in 1925; the Republic of Ararat, also in eastern Turkey, survived four years before being smothered in 1931.

In 1946, the U.S.S.R. sponsored another Kurdish state, the Republic of Mahabad, in northern Iran, hoping to destabilize the Shah's regime. The Soviets pulled out the following year, leaving their erstwhile clients to be massacred by the Iranians.

THIS MELANCHOLY THEME— powerful nations support the Kurds for tactical reasons, only to decide later that they are expendable—is a familiar pattern. It happened again in the 1970s, when the U.S. and Iran both urged Iraqi Kurds to rebel, as a means of pressuring Baghdad into concessions over access to a waterway on the Persian Gulf. After Iran and Iraq came to terms, the Kurds were abandoned and slaughtered once more; thousands died.

Turkey's Kurds have fared little better: nation-builder Mustafa Kemal Ataturk repressed them, and the Kurdish language was officially banned until 1991. The Partiya Karkaren Kurdistan, or P.K.K., is a militant group of Turkish Kurds founded by Abdullah Ocalan that fights for self-rule; it is regarded as a terrorist group by Turkey, the U.S. and the European Union. Turkey's government leveled some 3,000 Kurdish villages sympathetic to the P.K.K. cause during the 1980s and '90s, but the repression has lifted in recent years, thanks to European pressure.

Saddam Hussein persecuted Iraq's Kurds in the late 1980s, and again they became pawns in a game of political chess. In 1991 they rose up when President George H.W. Bush incited them to overthrow Saddam in the wake of the first Gulf War, but they were annihilated when Saddam fought back and the U.S. didn't intervene. More than 10,000 Kurds are thought to have died.

With the end of Saddam's regime, the Kurds of Iraq have reason to feed on hope once again. But they might do well to keep in mind a poignant saying coined by their ancestors: "Kurds have no friends. ■

Black Sea   GEORGIA
Ankara   ARMENIA   Baku
TURKEY   AZERBAIJAN   UZBEKISTAN
Ashgabat
KURD AREA   Caspian Sea
Nicosia   Mosul   IRAN
Mediterranean Sea   SYRIA   Tehran
Beirut
LEBANON   Damascus   Baghdad
ISRAEL
Jerusalem   Amman   IRAQ
Cairo   JORDAN   Basra
SAUDI ARABIA   KUWAIT

Kurd population:	
Turkey	14-22 million
Iran	5-6 million
Iraq	4-6 million
Syria	1-2 million

200 miles
200 km

Saddam's Wrath

Saddam Hussein viewed Iraq's 5 million Kurds as an alien, subversive group, and he sought to exterminate them after they took Iran's side in the long war between the two nations in the 1980s. "They collaborated against their own country," he declared. In the 1988 al-Anfal campaign, Saddam's military is believed to have slaughtered nearly 200,000 Kurdish civilians *(see page 96)*. Above, Saddam stands trial in July 2006 in Baghdad on charges of genocide for those deeds.

In today's occupied Iraq, the Kurdish regions in the north operate as semiautonomous entities under their own political leaders, and these provinces are among Iraq's most peaceful regions.

EXILES: Displaced in the fighting after the U.S. incursion in Iraq in 2003, Kurdish refugees set up camp outside the town of Dohuk

The Turks

REPUBLIC OF TURKEY

Population 68,893,918

Religion Sunni Muslim, 99%

Defining Moment Mustafa Kemal Ataturk chose to model his nation on the West in the 1920s; his reforms shaped modern Turkey

SUSPENDED BETWEEN ASIA AND Europe, Turkey has often been one of history's fulcrums. Like their ancestors, modern Turks are poised uneasily between old ways and new, Christianity and Islam, the Arab League and the European Union. Theirs is a Janus among nations.

Looking West, Turkey has been a staunch ally of the U.S.'s since the end of World War II; during the cold war, U.S. missiles stationed there were trained on Moscow. Under Prime Minister Recep Tayyip Erdogan, Turkey officially wants to keep its Western orientation. Struggling to meet tough criteria to be be accepted into the European Union, Ankara in recent years passed more than 40 laws and in excess of 300 articles to bring Turkish legislation and government structures in line with European norms. The death penalty has been abolished, press restrictions have been lifted, women have won new rights, and the overweening power of the country's military has been ratcheted down a bit.

Yet Turkey also looks east and south: it is almost 100% Muslim, and its faithful face Mecca five times a day to pray. With tensions high across Europe over the impact of the rising influx of Muslims into European nations, Turkey faces a tough battle to win full E.U. membership.

Among those questioning the idea was Joseph Cardinal Ratzinger, the conservative Vatican theologian, who in 2004 warned that admitting Muslim Turkey to the E.U. would threaten the Continent's "cultural richness." In 2006, as Pope Benedict XVI, Ratzinger's long-planned visit to Turkey was almost canceled after he delivered a speech in Germany that was interpreted in many Muslim lands as an attack on Islam.

TURKEY'S RELATIONS WITH THE U.S. have cooled since the run-up to the 2003 incursion into Iraq that toppled Saddam Hussein. When U.S. diplomats offered Turkey $6 billion in return for the right to use its military bases to help the effort, polls showed 90% of Turks opposed the plan, and Parliament voted down the deal.

Yet Turkey has also been on the receiving end of the recent upsurge in Islamic terrorism: more than 50 people were killed and hundreds

wounded in a series of 2003 bombings in Istanbul that are believed to be the work of al-Qaeda.

Turkey also faces a long-running internal dilemma over the fate of its 12 million Kurds, who make up almost 20% of the population. Again with an eye to a watching E.U., Ankara has toned down its struggle with the militant Kurdistan Workers' Party (P.K.K.) in recent years. Kurds who were once jailed for listening to Kurdish songs can now attend Kurdish language courses and watch Kurdish TV.

Which way will Turkey turn? In A.D. 1453, Constantinople fell to the armies of Islam, ending the Byzantine Empire and ushering in a new age in world affairs. More than 550 years later, it is no exaggeration to say that the direction the Turks choose to face may once again play an important role in shaping the future of the region. ∎

Turkey's Man in the Middle

Prime Minister Recep Erdogan is leading his nation's fight to be accepted into the European Union, despite the fact that he leads a conservative, pro-Islamic government. Erdogan was jailed in 1998 for violating Turkey's ban on the mixing of religion with politics after he recited a poem that compared minarets to bayonets. When his Justice and Development Party won power in 2002, Erdogan was unable to take office because of this conviction, until lawmakers passed a bill allowing him to do so. It was that experience, aides say, that convinced him that his party's political survival depended on European guarantees of freedom of expression. As a conservative Muslim, Erdogan is well placed to bring traditionalists with him on the issue of entering the E.U., a Turkish diplomat told TIME in 2004.

The Missing Caliph

Turkey reached perhaps its greatest influence in the wider world during the reign of Sultan Suleyman I, right, known as the Magnificent, who ruled the empire founded by the Ottoman Turks until his death in 1566. First appearing in the 13th century, the Ottoman Turks overran much of the Middle East, then trained their sights on Europe. They conquered Constantinople in 1453, ending the Byzantine Empire, then took control of much of the Balkans. Their path of conquest was finally turned back at Vienna in 1683.

As in most Islamic nations, there was no distinction between state and church in the Ottoman Empire; during the 600 years of its existence, Muslims everywhere looked to the sultan and caliph in Constantinople as Islam's highest authorities in political and spiritual life.

When Mustafa Kemal Ataturk set out to modernize Turkey in the wake of World War I, he overthrew both the sultanate and caliphate. Since that time, Muslims have lacked a single religious figure who can speak for all of them. One of the primary goals of Osama bin Laden, as stated in his writings and speeches, is to restore the role and primacy of the lost caliphate and thus unite the Islamic world.

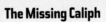

CROSSROADS: Since Ataturk's reforms, Turkey has become highly Westernized, as this picture of the Leb-i Derya Cafe in Istanbul shows: women without scarves mingle freely with men, and alcohol is legal

The Afghans

ISLAMIC EMIRATE OF AFGHANISTAN

Population: 28,513,677

Religion: Sunni, 80%; Shi'ite ,19%

Defining Moment: A U.S.-led coalition freed the nation from the Taliban in 2001, but the militants are rebuilding their forces

RUDYARD KIPLING DIDN'T shrink from the horrors of colonial warfare in his 1892 poem "The Young British Soldier":

When you're wounded and left on Afghanistan's plains
And the women come out to cut up what remains
Jest roll on your rifle an' blow out your brains
An' go to your Gawd like a soldier.

Kipling knew Britain's troops: the foot soldiers fielded by the greatest superpower of the 19th century dreaded duty in Afghanistan. The duel between Britain and Russia for dominance in Central Asia, to which Afghanistan's Khyber Pass held the key, was termed the "great game." But it was a bloody, exhausting contest, and both powers were eventually humbled there, earning Afghanistan the grim sobriquet "graveyard of empires."

The British got their comeuppance in the mid-1800s: in 1842 a column of 16,500 retreating soldiers was reduced in seven days to a single survivor by the harrying Afghans. The Russians learned their lesson in the 1980s. Both discovered too late that the country's topography, a captivating tableau of high mountains, deep valleys and wide plains, is perfect for guerrilla warfare. Here, knowledge of the terrain is the most important weapon an army can have.

NO IRON FIST, NOT EVEN THAT OF THE Taliban, has ever succeeded in fully unifying this nation of five major ethnic and cultural groups—Pashtuns, Tajiks, Hazaras, Uzbeks and Turkmans—who speak eight major languages as well as 30 minor dialects. Only one cause seems to have ever united Afghans: resistance to foreign invaders. That instinct has deep roots in Afghan history: Alexander the Great first stumbled here, and Genghis Khan found it easier to reach accommodations with the Afghans than to conquer them.

Although it has often humbled great powers, Afghanistan, landlocked and impoverished, has never been powerful. Riven by factionalism and dominated by regional warlords, Afghanistan's various tribes and clans have little in common other than their religion: most are Sunni Muslims, and for centuries, many Afghans have labored to halt the eastward spread of neighboring Iran's despised Shi'ite sect.

IN 2001 A NEW GROUP OF OUTSIDERS, a U.S.-led allied coalition, drove the Taliban from power and presided over the installation of Pashtun chief Hamid Karzai as the nation's President. But in the years since, the allies have tangled with the nation's warlords and fought to keep the Taliban, many of whom retreated to the remote border region with Pakistan, from regrouping. Karzai's grasp on

A Good Neighbor? Musharraf's Plight

Since coming to power in a military coup in 1999, Pakistan's President, Pervez Musharraf, has occupied one of the hottest seats in the world. The 9/11 attacks on the U.S. forced Musharraf to choose between his people—many of whom sympathize with the cause of Islamism and the radical Taliban in neighboring Afghanistan—and his allies in Washington. Musharraf chose the latter, cooperating with the 2001 coalition that toppled the Taliban, but he continues to walk a fine line. He has blocked U.S. troops from Pakistan's historically autonomous Federally Administered Tribal Areas along the Afghanistan-Pakistan border, where al-Qaeda's top leaders are believed to be hiding. In August 2006 an internal crisis rocked Pakistan, when government security forces killed Nawab Akbar Khan Bugti, a leader in the ongoing rebellion of the nation's large ethnic minority, the Baluchs. Bugti was a former provincial governor and chief minister and the moderate leader of a respected political party. With his death, Musharraf will face rising pressures from within, to match the pressures outside—from the U.S. and its allies, and from extremists on his borders.

power doesn't extend far into the countryside, and as of 2006, the war to control Afghanistan's future is very much unresolved.

Reporting from Zabul province in Afghanistan's south in September 2006, TIME's Aryn Baker found that Taliban forces were growing bolder in the region, where a unit of NATO troops had recently taken over from U.S. soldiers assigned to keep peace. Ironically, the region had once been touted as the allied coalition's success story in the south. A U.S.-led provincial reconstruction project had resulted in the building of a new hospital, a women's center, a job-training facility and a new bank.

In recent weeks, Baker reported, Taliban checkpoints had been set up in several places along the region's main highway, and trucks transporting goods had been detained. Taliban fighters had begun attacking Afghan police officers and troops, while coalition soldiers had seen a major increase in the number of improvised bombs, ambushes and mortar attacks they had to endure.

Five years after the coalition routed the Taliban, the militants were returning to haunt their nation, and Kipling was looking as much like a prophet as a poet. ∎

A Bumper Crop for Warlords—and the Taliban

During their five years in power, the Taliban were more successful than any previous Afghan government in crushing the cultivation of opium poppies, the plant from which heroin is derived. While in power, the Taliban scorned the drug, though the opium crop has long been a primary source of revenue for the nation's warlords and farmers. But the Taliban's 2001 fall, and the subsequent flow of power to local warlords, has reopened the floodgates, and Afghanistan has resumed its traditional role as the world's largest supplier of heroin. Opium revenue amounts to some 35% of the nation's gross domestic product.

Despite a high-profile attempt by U.S. and officials in Kabul to eradicate producers, Afghanistan's 2006 harvest was reported to be the largest in history. United Nations authorities predicted it would amount to 6,100 tons, 92% of the world supply. Remnants of the Taliban have changed their tune:, now relegated to the status of guerrillas, they have struck up a marriage of mutual convenience with the narcotics farmers they once terrorized: drug lords funnel money and arms to the Islamic insurgents, in exchange for protection. Afghanistan's 2006 bumper crop of opium is good news for the Taliban.

FLOWER POWER: Farmers bring in the poppy harvest outside Kandahar in 2002

The Gulf States

WHILE IT'S EASY TO GROUP the various smaller countries of the Arabian Peninsula into a single entity—a temptation we've succumbed to here—each of these modern nations has its own identity, history and culture, and stark differences distinguish them.

The states located directly on the Persian Gulf, home of the world's largest reserves of oil, have shared in the gusher of petrodollars that has also transformed the dominant regional nation, Saudi Arabia. One exception: Dubai, the leading member of the United Arab Emirates (U.A.E.), lost out in the geological jackpot; only 6% of its economy is oil-based. Not to worry: Dubai is thriving as a major player in world trade. On its shores, as on those of its neighbors, dazzling modern buildings have arisen in recent years.

Forging a partnership that has endured, the Persian Gulf nations of Bahrain, Kuwait, Oman, Qatar and the U.A.E. joined Saudi Arabia in 1981 to form the Cooperation Council for the Arab States of the Gulf. Yemen is seeking membership in the council, which coordinates social, economic and scientific development in the region.

ON THE FAR SOUTH OF THE ARABIAN Peninsula, on the Gulf of Aden, lies another nation that hasn't shared in the petroleum bonanza, Yemen. Its gross domestic product (GDP) in 2005 was $16 billion; per capita income was $800. In contrast, Saudi Arabia's GDP was $310 billion; per capita income was $10,000. Yemen's poverty and relatively weak government have made it a familiar stopping point on the terrorist trail. The U.S.S. *Cole* was bombed in the port city of Aden in 2000. Less well remembered is the bombing of a French oil tanker, the *Limburg*, off the country's coast in 2002. The government of President Abdullah Ali Saleh has been battling a major internal Islamist militant group, the Aden-Abyan Islamic Army, which kidnapped 16 Western tourists in 1998-99; four hostages died in an ill-conceived rescue attempt.

Saleh maintains strict control over television and other media; in March 2006, he temporarily shut down the nation's foremost independent newspaper, the *Yemen Observer*. Saleh, who was elected in 1999 and re-elected in September 2006, has pledged to work with the U.S. in combatting terrorism, but U.S. investigators dispatched to Yemen in the wake of the *Cole* bombing reported that the government hampered their efforts.

On Feb. 2, 2006, 23 convicted al-Qaeda members being held in a single room in a Yemeni jail escaped. "We are disappointed that their restrictions in prison weren't more stringent," said U.S. counterterrorism czar Frances Fragos Townsend. When asked why the U.S. wasn't keeping closer tabs on the prisoners' incarceration, a U.S. law enforcement official replied, "that assumes the Yemenis care what we think." ∎

Thanks to Petrodollars, Architecture on Steroids

The immense oil riches of the Middle East have created a society of instant boomtowns, as entire cultures seem to have traded camels for Jaguars in the course of two or three generations, leaving whole centuries in the rearview mirror. One result: architects are enjoying the opportunity to build enormous and often cutting-edge sructures there. Among the most recognizable is the hotel at right, the Burj al-Arab (Arabian Tower), designed by Briton Tom Wright, in Dubai in the United Arab Emirates. Opened in 1999 and built on an artificial island, the hotel takes its shape from the sail of an ancient Arab dhow. It boasts such amenities as a lily-pad heliport on top and an underwater restaurant, accessible only by submarine.

The Kuwait Towers in Kuwait City, left, date from 1979; they serve as water towers and utility centers, but the tallest tower also contains a restaurant and rotating observation deck in the largest sphere—further proof that the oil wealth of the gulf is enough to make your head spin.

ARAB SPIRE: The Burj al-Arab hotel has become a worldwide tourist attraction since it opened in 2004. Tiger Woods used its heliport as a driving range

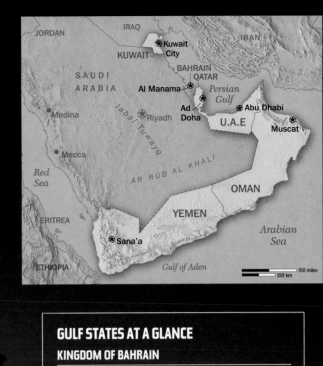

GULF STATES AT A GLANCE

KINGDOM OF BAHRAIN

Capital Manamah   **Population** 688,345

Religions Shi'ite, 70%; Sunni, 30%

In Brief Bahrain, a longtime British protectorate, did not achieve independence until 1971. The archipelago kingdom is a close ally of the U.S.'s in the region.

STATE OF KUWAIT

Capital Kuwait City   **Population** 2,335, 648

Religions Muslim, 85%, mainly Sunni; Christian, Hindu, 15%

In Brief The U.S. ally has seen an uptick in Islamic fundamentalism in recent years, but in 2005 it gave women the right to vote.

SULTANATE OF OMAN

Capital Muscat   **Population** 3,001,583

Religions Ibadhi Muslim, 75%; other Muslim sects, 20%

In Brief This isolated nation, once an oligarchy, has extended suffrage to all, including women.

STATE OF QATAR

Capital Doha   **Population** 863,051

Religion Muslim, 95%

In Brief The tiny, oil-rich former British protectorate is home to the controversial TV network al-Jazeera. A relatively liberal Arab state, it is a U.S. ally.

UNITED ARAB EMIRATES

Capital Abu Dhabi   **Population** 2,563,212

Religions Sunni, 80%; Shi'ite, 16%; Christian, Hindu, 4%

In Brief The federation of seven emirates was formed in 1971. The U.S. ally was used by al-Qaeda for funds shipments before 9/11 but later froze those accounts.

REPUBLIC OF YEMEN

Capital Sana'a   **Population** 20,727,063

Religions Islam, 98%

In Brief Once two nations, one a strong ally of Moscow's, Yemen was unified in 1990 but has seen much civil strife in recent years. It is a hotbed of Islamist militancy and site of the U.S.S. *Cole* bombing in 2000.

Source: TIME Almanac

The Middle East in Modern Times

For long centuries, the West viewed the Middle East as deeply other and deeply exotic; Palestinian scholar Edward Said called that Western mirage "Orientalism." In the the 20th century, events began bringing the Middle East, Europe and the U.S. together. The aftershocks of that great collision are still being felt: they brought terrorism to American soil and sent U.S. soldiers to Afghanistan and Iraq. Three seminal events—the creation of new nations in the region after World War I, the discovery of oil riches and the birth of Israel—are the driving factors in this story so clotted with conflicts and crises.

World War I Creates New Nations

■ The Ottoman Empire chooses the wrong side in World War I, and at the war's end, European powers draw up a new map of the Middle East, creating nations that do not reflect local cultures

LESS THAN A MONTH AFTER SEPT. 11, 2001, A VIDEO-tape surfaced in which Osama bin Laden tried to justify the terrorist attacks he had launched at the U.S.: "Our Islamic world has been tasting the same humiliation and disgrace for more than 80 years," he said. The reference mystified most Western listeners, but not the Muslim world: he was referring to the fall of the Ottoman Caliphate, symbol of the unity of Islam, after World War I. That war's conclusion led to a series of tectonic shifts in the political landscape that created a new map of the Middle East.

The first rumble of this political earthquake was the tragic miscalculation by the Ottoman Empire to take Germany's side in the war, mainly because the Germans were at war with the Ottomans' traditional enemy, Russia. By 1916, as the war was turning against the Central Powers, the Allies (chiefly Britain and France) began to negotiate the Sykes-Picot Agreement, a secret deal to divvy up the Ottoman Empire, which stretched from present-day Turkey to the lands we now call Lebanon, Syria, Palestine and Israel, to Saudi Arabia, Yemen, Qatar, Kuwait and Iraq, and beyond to Bahrain and the United Arab Emirates.

The Ottomans had ruled most of these territories for centuries, some for more than a thousand years. By the early 1900s, however, the empire was in the final stages of a long decline; World War I finished it off. Turkey, its last remnant, emerged from the ruins as a newly independent nation.

Carving up the spoils under Sykes-Picot, England tightened its grip on Egypt (already a British colony) and also took control of Palestine, Iraq, various gulf states and Transjordan, today's Jordan. France received Lebanon and Syria. Those moves reneged on promises of postwar independence that had been made to various Arab chieftains by the British representative in the region, T.E. Lawrence. They also ignored the religious, tribal, ethnic and historic divisions that mean everything in the Middle East. Many of the new nations created by Sykes-Picot are bordered by neat, straight lines—and that's a problem. They reflect not natural frontiers—rivers and mountains—but demarcations drawn up at a European conference table by colonial authorities who knew little and cared less about the region's history and culture.

Iraq and Lebanon are two cases in point. The latter was carved out of territory traditionally ruled from the Syrian capital of Damascus, explaining why Syria to this day attempts to control events within Lebanon. Iraq was cobbled together from a jumble of mutually antagonistic factions: Shi'ites, Sunnis and Kurds. Adding fuel to the fire, in the 1920s the British carved out part of the territory historically controlled by Baghdad and created another independent nation, Kuwait.

U.S. President Woodrow Wilson called World War I "the war to end all wars." British colonial governor Archibald Wavell assayed the war's impact on the Middle East more trenchantly when he said the Allies had wrought "a peace to end all peace." The decades to come would prove Wavell the better prophet. ■

DELEGATES: Arab representatives gather at the Versailles Peace Conference in 1919. At front is Faisal, briefly King of Syria and later Iraq. Behind him, left to right: Faisal's aide Rustem Haidar; future Iraqi leader Nuri Said; Captain Rosario Pisani of France; T. E. Lawrence ("Lawrence of Arabia"); and Hassan Khadri, Faisal's military advisor. At rear: Faisal's African slave

MARCHING ORDERS: Ataturk addresses followers in 1923

1923

Ataturk Modernizes Turkey

■ Turkey, which lies like a bridge between two cultures, turns its gaze to the West after World War I, following the vision of a great leader

EXPLAINING HIS POLITICAL PHILOSOPHY TO A mystified Western reporter, Mustafa Kemal Ataturk once declared, "I am dictating democracy to my people." And he meant it. A strongman who was the equal of Joseph Stalin or Saddam Hussein in the sway he exercised over his people, Ataturk was unlike those despots in that exerted his enormous power largely to benevolent ends.

A military hero who bested the Allies at Gallipoli three times during World War I, then repelled an invading Greek army (sponsored by the British) to salvage the Turkish nation from the ruins of the Ottoman Empire, Ataturk was Turkey's indispensable man. He had the charisma and moral authority to lead an entire nation on a radical new course, turning its orientation from the ancient ways of the Middle East and toward Western modernity.

In a 1928 speech, Ataturk recalled the triumphs of his regime: the sultan overthrown, the Turkish republic proclaimed, the Ottoman Caliphate unseated, polygamy abolished, the fez banned, women unveiled and a new capital, Ankara, built at ancient Angora.

Appalled that 80% of his people were illiterate in Arabic, Ataturk asked a commission how long it would take Turkey to adopt the Latin alphabet. When the response was five years, Ataturk decreed that it would happen "in three months or it will not happen at all." He was wrong: it took just over two months to convert all government documents and most business offices to the new alphabet. Within a year, more than 1 million Turks had learned to read and write with the new letters.

Ataturk also closed religious courts and schools, established a new public education system and rejected Shari'a, enacting a new code of civil law based on that used by Switzerland and Germany. His final reform, undertaken in 1935, three years before his death, was to adopt surnames for every Turk, who previously had identified themselves only by a given name. Born Mustafa and nicknamed Kemal ("Perfection") by an elementary school teacher for his proficiency in algebra, Turkey's President allowed the Parliament to select his last name. It chose Ataturk, which means "Father of the Turks."

Ataturk admired democracy in theory more than in practice, once saying, "Liberty is like fire. It's beneficent if controlled, but abandoned to itself, it burns and destroys." Nor did he hesitate to use Turkey's army (and, more than a few times, the gallows) to enforce his will.

Yet unlike Iran's Shah Reza Pahlavi, who tried to cram centuries of modernization down the throats of his people in a single generation only to reap the whirlwind, Ataturk somehow got it right. After his 1938 death, Turkey continued on the course he had set for it, holding free, multiparty elections for the first time in 1950. Long one of the few secular nations in the Middle East, it still turns its face to the West, although, thanks to Islam's fundamentalist revival of recent years, the call of the muezzin is sounding more appealing to the ears of some of today's young Turks. ■

1948

Birth of Israel

■ Zionism's appeal and Europe's unrest send long-scattered Jews flocking to their ancient homeland, but when the nation of Israel is born at last, Palestine's Arabs are displaced as refugees

A LITERAL READING OF THE BIBLE INDICATES THAT God gave Abraham title to everything between Egypt and Iraq sometime in the Bronze Age. The *Book of Genesis* declares, "The Lord made a covenant with Abraham, saying, Unto thy seed have I given this land, from the river of Egypt unto the great river, the river Euphrates." That was the Promised Land.

For a few precious centuries, Jews thrived in their homeland in Israel. But that nation fell, and its people went into the exile of the Diaspora. For 2,000 years the thought of Zion, (a mountain near Jerusalem in biblical times), warmed the minds of the world's scattered Jews. "Next year in Jerusalem"—the words

ended in an ardent sigh in Europe's shtetls and ghettos. Finally, a few decades after the dreams of European Jews to return to Israel began coalescing to form the movement known as Zionism, Jews were given a new deed to the land, if by a slightly less divine hand than that of Yahweh: the British Empire.

The new deed was the Balfour Declaration, issued in 1917 by Foreign Secretary Arthur Balfour. "His Majesty's Government," it said, "views with favor the establishment in Palestine of a national home for the Jewish people, and will use their best endeavors to facilitate the achievement of this object." (Israelis tend to quote this first part of the declaration, while Arabs recall with bitterness the following proviso: "... it being clearly understood that nothing shall be done which may prejudice the civil and religious rights of existing non-Jewish communities in Palestine.")

When the League of Nations formally handed the governance of Palestine to Britain in 1922, the mandate specifically endorsed the Balfour Declaration, although the declaration contradicted agreements British representatives had made with Arab leaders during the war. The British also created a new nation in the region, Transjordan, on the eastern bank of the Jordan River, which amount-

ed to some 80% of the old Palestine; Jews and western Palestinians were barred from settling in this new nation.

Since the 1890s, European Jews had been immigrating to Palestine, fired by Zionist dreams and fleeing pogroms and discrimination. The emigrations, or aliyahs, took place in a series of waves; by 1925 there were 160,000 Jews in Palestine. As Arabs claimed their lands were being overrun by foreigners, Britain clamped down on Jewish immigration. As tensions rose, Arabs rioted in Jerusalem and elsewhere. In response, the Jews created an underground military organization, the Haganah, to protect themselves.

In 1939 Britain issued a white paper repudiating the Balfour Declaration and shutting off all Jewish immigration to Palestine—just as World War II was beginning to create millions of Jewish refugees in Europe. In response, Palestine's Jews turned to terrorism against the British rulers: two groups, the Lehi and Irgun, began a campaign of bombing British offices and police stations. The British hit back hard, ratcheting up the tension.

By 1946, with the war ended, Palestine was a war zone, with the British and Jews openly battling. On July 22, 1946, Irgun agents

BATTLES: Left, on Jan. 1, 1947, the *Theodor Herzl*, bearing Jewish refugees from Europe after World War II, waits outside a Palestine port; the British barred it from landing. Above, Jewish soldiers on May 20, 1948, a week after independence

led by Menachem Begin bombed the British headquarters in Jerusalem, the King David Hotel, killing 91 people. By 1947, the British had had enough: they took their problem child to the new United Nations, which created a plan to partition Palestine into two nations, one for Jews, one for Arabs. Jerusalem was to be designated an international city under U.N. control. Most Jews accepted the plan, if reluctantly; the Palestinians and other Arabs utterly rejected it.

The Jews in Palestine had an important ally in Washington. Deeply affected by the Holocaust, President Harry Truman sympathized with their aspirations for a homeland. In November 1947 he lobbied in the U.N. for the partition plan, and it passed. But the British refused to impose the plan, because of the Arabs' rejection, and they declared they would evacuate Palestine on May 15, 1948.

Jews in Palestine now took matters into their own hands. At 4 p.m. on May 14, moderate Jewish leader David Ben-Gurion read a 979-word declaration of independence in front a of small audience at the Tel Aviv Art Museum. He finished, "The state of Israel is established! The meeting is ended." At midnight, British rule over Palestine lapsed: 11 minutes later White House spokesman Charlie Ross announced U.S. recognition.

At the moment of its birth, Israel was fighting for its life, as the neighboring Arab states tried to annihilate the alien creation in its midst. Even As Ben-Gurion was making his announcement, five Arab armies—from Transjordan, Egypt, Syria, Lebanon and Iraq—were poised to invade the new Jewish state.

In the war of independence that followed, the physical proximities of the land, and the hatreds that filled them, were terrifying. Arabs and Jews stared into one another's gun muzzles. The corridor from the Mediterranean coast to Jerusalem was constantly vulnerable—and still is littered with the charred shells of trucks and armored cars destroyed as Israel's fledgling army struggled to relieve the besieged Jews of Jerusalem (the wreckage left as a monument and cautionary tale). Three-quarters of the Jewish population and all of Israel's major cities, its airports and the bulk of its industry lay within range of Arab artillery. The Israelis dug in and survived.

The war dragged on for months, bleeding both sides, until all parties accepted a U.N. truce in December 1948. The Israelis held a C-shaped majority of the land that ran from Galilee in the north to the Sinai peninsula in the south, leaving the Arabs only a central "ear" from Jerusalem east to the Jordan River and the tiny sliver of Gaza, placed under Egypt's control. Transjordan took over the Old City of Jerusalem, site of Judaism's great shrine, the Western Wall, and the West Bank area of the Jordan River (and soon changed its name to Jordan). Hundreds of thousands of Palestinian Arabs fled their villages for Jordan, for Gaza, for the West Bank, for other Arab countries. Many landed in squalid refugee camps, where they live now.

The Zionist dream cracked apart just when it seemed to have been achieved. "A land without people for a people without land," said the hopeful Zionist formula. But Palestine was not a "land without people," and the Jewish state from its birth has lived in a state of war in order to protect the dream from the discrepancy. ■

1953

RETURN OF THE KING: Pro-Shah Iranians herald
the young man's return to his country on Aug. 1, 1953

A U.S. Coup in Iran

■ When Iran's leader nationalizes Britain's oil operations, the U.S. sponsors his overthrow and brings a Western-oriented regime to the petroleum-rich nation

DEPENDING ON YOUR POLITICAL POINT OF VIEW, Mohammed Mossadegh was either a visionary statesman or an unprincipled troublemaker. Either way, the man Iranians chose in 1951 as their first democratically elected Prime Minister was an impassioned orator who had long chafed at Britain's domination of Iran's oil reserves. The Anglo-Iranian Oil Co., a predecessor of today's British Petroleum, held the concession for all of Iran, handing back only a token share of the proceeds. Mossadegh wanted a fifty-fifty split, then becoming the standard deal between oil-rich Middle Eastern nations and U.S. companies. When the British refused, Mossadegh nationalized the company.

The British called his bluff, boycotting Iranian oil, and the U.S. joined them. No international oil company would buy Iran's oil. The Iranians had no system for delivering it or the technical skills to produce it, since the British had long relegated Iranian workers to menial jobs. Mossadegh threatened to flood the world with half-price oil, yet he could deliver only a trickle because of the blockade. As Iran's government withered, the Eisenhower Administration cut off foreign aid. Unrest followed, and angry citizens took to the streets, prompting fears that the communists were plotting to move in, even though Mossadegh hated the Soviets just as much as the British.

On Aug. 19, 1953, after

Mossadegh in 1953

the deaths of some 300 people in street riots, the 71-year-old Premier was overthrown and replaced by retired army general Fazollah Zahedi. The American-friendly Shah, Mohammed Reza Pahlavi, who had earlier fled the country, returned in triumph, resumed the Peacock Throne and reasserted his control.

In truth, the regime change was anything but spontaneous. It was orchestrated by the CIA, under the code name "Operation Ajax." Longtime intelligence agent Kermit Roosevelt, a grandson of Theodore Roosevelt's, and U.S. Army General H. Norman Schwarzkopf, the father of the general who would lead the liberation of Kuwait in 1991, ran the show.

U.S. operatives paid Iranian newspaper editors to print anti-Mossadegh stories, secured the cooperation of the Iranian military and spread antigovernment rumors. They prepared false documents that depicted secret agreements between Mossadegh and the local Communist Party. They masqueraded as communists, threatened conservative Muslim clerics and even staged a sham, harmless fire bombing of the home of a religious leader. They also stage-managed the appearance of Mossadegh's successor, General Zahedi, whose personal bank account they fattened.

With Mossadegh gone, British Petroleum returned to the Iranian oil fields. Some newcomers tagged along: five U.S.companies, the ancestors of today's ExxonMobil and Chevron-Texaco. Meanwhile, a relieved U.S. government opened the foreign-aid spigot. Over the next 25 years, more than $20 billion in U.S. funds would pour into a decidedly undemocratic Iran, most of it in the form of military aid and subsidized weapons sales for the Shah's armed forces and SAVAK, his dreaded secret police. As for U.S. oil companies, they would extract 2 billion bbl. of oil from their new Iranian fields. But that access carried a stiff price tag. The Shah's oppression led to the founding of the first Western-hating Islamic republic, when the Shi'ite clerics duped by the CIA's 1953 coup staged their own power grab in 1979, placing Ayatullah Ruhollah Khomeini in charge of a newly militant Iran. ■

The Shah returns to Iran

Shah Reza Pahlavi

Like many Iranians, he dreamed of restoring his country to its days of imperial grandeur; unlike them, he was able foster this dream. The tragedy of Shah Reza Pahlavi's life is that he did both too little and too much in pursuing that quest.

The Shah was seated on the Peacock Throne in 1941 at age 21, installed by the British, who suspected his father of Nazi sympathies. For years, the young ruler was treated as a vassal by his patrons in the U.S. and Britain. After the war, however, Iran became a cold war prize—both because Russia was training an acquisitive eye on its warm-water ports on the Persian Gulf and because the country sat atop underground oceans of oil.

Propped up by billions in petrodollars and billions more in U.S. military aid, the Shah spent lavishly, transforming Iran into a thriving regional, if not quite global, power. Fearful of Soviet subversion, however, and insecure in his grip on power, the Shah kept Iran's political processes in the Dark Ages. He ruled as an absolute monarch: his citizens had few rights, and his opponents feared for their lives. By the late 1970s, the longing for liberty and the social dislocation created by sudden change made Iranians ripe for exploitation by a fundamentalist cleric who preached a return to the sanctity of traditional ways.

A Man, a Plan, a Canal: Suez

■ Egypt's aggressive new leader, Gamal Abdel Nasser, battles Britain, France and Israel over control of the Suez. And the U.S., in a surprise that alters the world's balance of power, backs away from its allies

THE MAN WAS EGYPT'S VIBRANT YOUNG LEADER, Gamal Abdel Nasser, who brought a surge of Arab nationalism to his country after masterminding the 1952 army coup that overthrew hereditary monarch King Farouk, a close British ally. Nasser's plan was bold: he would wrench a hated symbol of Western colonialism, the Suez Canal, away from its proprietors, Britain and France, nationalizing a bulwark of European power in the Middle East. In the end, Nasser's power play would prove pivotal for not only the region but also the world's balance of power.

Determined to rebuild his nation, Nasser hoped to draw power from his planned Aswan High Dam along the Nile. Playing off cold war rivalries, he sought the support of both the U.S. and U.S.S.R. to finance it. The U.S. originally agreed to do so but, alarmed by Nasser's courtship of Moscow, withdrew its offer.

A week later, on July 26, 1956, Nasser stunned the world and thrilled his people when he declared he would expel all British troops from Egypt and would nationalize the Suez Canal. Built by the French and opened in 1869, the canal was intended to speed ships directly from Europe to India and Asia, bypassing the African continent. By the 1950s it served an even more vital function, connecting the rich oil fields of the Arabian peninsula with Europe.

Nasser had a secondary goal in mind: the humbling of his hated neighbor, Israel. Along his border, Palestinian refugees, displaced by the birth of Israel in 1948, had been settling in the Gaza Strip, a narrow slice of land along the Mediterranean that was a part of the former British Mandate of Palestine but was now under Egypt's control. In 1955, Nasser began sending the fedayeen, peasant-guerrillas, to join Palestinians in crossing from Gaza into

DIRE STRAITS: An Arab ship, struck by French bombs, sinks in the Suez Canal in 1956. After the Anglo-French invasion, Nasser ordered the sinking of all 40 British and French ships then present in the canal. The crisis closed the vital commercial route to all shipping until 1957

Israel to hector the Israeli settlers in the area.

As Britain and France considered their response to Nasser's ploy, they brought Israel—the enemy of their enemy, Egypt—into their deliberations. The plan they hatched gave the crisis the name by which it's known in the Arab world: the Tripartite Aggression.

On Oct. 29, Israel invaded the Gaza Strip and the Sinai Peninsula, launching a full-scale war with Egypt, and kicking off a plan agreed upon days before in Sèvres, France. Per that plan, British Prime Minister Anthony Eden and French Prime Minister Guy Mollet quickly made an offer to Nasser: they would dispatch troops to the region, occupy the territory and separate the warring armies. Their real aim, of course, was to regain control of the canal. In short, the two European powers colluded with Israel to begin a war intended to teach Nasser a lesson and take back the canal.

Nasser refused the British and French offer, as they had expected he would: now they had a pretext to invade the region. And invade they did, having marshaled major naval and air forces off Egypt's Mediterranean coast. Under Operation Musketeer, the two powers began bombing Egypt on Oct. 31; a D-day-style parachute drop and beach invasion at Port Said at the canal's northern end followed on Nov. 5

and 6. Meanwhile, Israeli troops and tanks routed Egypt's army in the Sinai Peninsula, advancing south along the peninsula as far as Sharm el-Sheikh, at its tip.

Israel, France and Britain assumed their strike would be supported by the U.S. But President Dwight Eisenhower was infuriated by the scheming of the three allies: to the surprise of the world, he sided with Moscow, condemning the war, calling for an immediate cease-fire and embracing Canadian diplomat Lester Pearson's plan to send a U.N. peacekeeping force to the region. Israel withdrew from its conquered Egyptian territories but retained the right to send ships through the canal. As for Britain's Eden, he resigned in disgrace.

The Suez crisis was one of history's turning points: it demonstrated that two superpowers, the U.S. and U.S.S.R., now dominated global politics. It marked the ongoing decline of European influence in the Middle East, even as it spurred nascent pride among Arab nations and peoples. It distanced the U.S. from Israel for several years, and France stepped in as the young nation's major ally. The Suez crisis also showed that the U.S. was prepared to exert its influence to retain its access to Middle Eastern oil, which was now viewed by Washington as a vital U.S. security interest. ∎

Nasser in 1954

Gamal Abdel Nasser

A burly, broad-shouldered army officer, son of a lower-middle-class postal clerk, Gamal Abdel Nasser overturned Egypt's rotting monarchy in 1952 and brought visions of prosperity to his own country and hope for new unity to a diffuse and frustrated Arab world. He carried out drastic land reforms, wiping out a parasitic pasha class that had lived off the poverty-stricken peasants for generations. His defiance of Britain and France in the 1956 Suez crisis was a declaration of independence from the last vestiges of European colonialism.

Although he envisioned himself as the unifying leader of a new pan-Arab world, Nasser's 1958 political union with Syria, the United Arab Republic, proved a failure, and he precipitated a succession of feuds and intrigues with virtually every one of Egypt's Arab neighbors. At odds with Europe and the U.S., he turned to the Soviet bloc to rebuild his army and finance his long-time dream, the Aswan High Dam, but the alliance offered little to his people. He was humiliatingly trounced in two wars with Israel, the Six-Day War and the Yom Kippur War.

For all his shortcomings, Nasser managed one inestimable accomplishment. To the people of Egypt and the rest of the Arab world, he imparted a sense of personal worth and national pride that they had not known for 400 years.

Enter the P.L.O.—and Arafat

■ Years after the Arabs refused a U.N. plan that would have given Palestinians their own nation at Israel's birth, the refugees create a political arm designed to advance their cause

"PALESTINE IS THE CEMENT THAT HOLDS THE ARAB world together," Yasser Arafat told TIME in November 1974, "or it is the explosive that blows it apart." If the chief of the Palestine Liberation Organization (P.L.O.) was often accused of bending the facts in his decades-long career, he never spoke truer words than these. From the moment their diaspora began in 1948, the fate of the Palestinian people has been one of the foremost challenges confronting the Middle East—an ongoing goad to Islamic jihad and a source of constant irritation to Israel and its neighbors.

The first pages in this ongoing drama were written when Palestinians rejected the U.N. Partition plan, then failed to beat Israel in the war of 1948—*al-Nakbar,* the catastrophe, as they called it. Even so, in the first years after Israel's founding, there was a widespread sense among Arabs, Palestinians especially, that the Zionist boil in their midst would soon be lanced. There were just too many Arabs united by the common desire to drive the Jews out of the region for the tide of history not to turn in their favor. But as the years passed, and a second war, the 1956 Suez crisis, turned out badly for the Arab side, that goal began to seem more and more remote.

Around this time, in 1959, a Palestinian engineer living in Kuwait joined a handful of close friends to form a new resistance organization. Yasser Arafat and his comrades decided to call their guerrilla group Harakat al

GUERRILLAS: By 1968 the P.L.O. was running training camps in Jordan, below. Two years later King Hussein drove the militant group out of his country

Yasser Arafat

Take your pick: Yasser Arafat was either a murderer and a terrorist who should have been put on trial for his crimes and publicly executed—or he was a hero and nation builder, the George Washington of the Palestinians. If those polarities seem to offer no room for a middle ground, well, welcome to the Middle East.

Conniving yet disarming, sincere yet duplicitous, winner of the Nobel Peace Prize yet terror kingpin: the list of Arafat's contradictions is a long one. Yet it was Arafat who helped make the intellectual leap to a definition of the Palestinians as a distinct people. He articulated their cause, fought for it and brought it to the world's attention as no Kurd or Basque ever managed to do. He was the man Yitzhak Rabin dueled with for many years in many capacities—and yet he was the man whose hand Rabin, as Israel's Prime Minister, finally clasped at the White House in 1993, when the Palestine Liberation Organization was accepted into the world community.

As a boy growing up in Jerusalem and Cairo, the son of a spice merchant and grocer, Arafat had no revolutionary ambitions. After graduating from Cairo University, he went to Kuwait to make his fortune in construction. By age 30 he was a rich man, driving a Thunderbird, moving smoothly through the prosperous circles of Palestinian exiles and preparing to launch his crusade for their future.

His Fatah organization, which he founded in the late 1950s with other educated, well-to-do Palestinians, eventually became the heart of the P.L.O. During the first few years, he had the most to fear from other Arabs: he came

HIDING OUT: The guerrilla in 1970, roosting in a cave in Jordan

to know his way around the jails of Syria and Egypt, though Israel never once held him in prison. By the 1960s, Fatah was divided into two factions. There were the "sane ones," who urged building up the infant group before launching guerrilla attacks against Israel. And there were the "mad ones," already out for blood: Arafat was their leader. Whether he gave the orders or not, his organization was linked to some of the bloodiest acts of terrorism in the Arab-Israeli conflict, including the massacre of Israeli athletes at the 1972 Munich Olympics and the murder of hundreds of Israeli settlers in years of cross-border raids.

In his long career, Arafat and his cohort hunkered down in—and were thrown out of—a string of host nations: Jordan, then Lebanon, then Tunisia. By the early 1990s, Arafat had lost both his Soviet sponsors and his oil-rich Arab backers, who were upset by his support for Iraq in the Gulf War, while young Palestinians were rallying around Hamas, not Fatah. When a chance for legitimacy was offered in 1993, Arafat seized Rabin's hand like a lifeline. ■

Tahrir al-Falastin, or "Movement for the Liberation of Palestine." The clumsy name soon gave way to an acronym, Fatah, the Arabic word for "conquest," as well as its word for "death" when spelled backwards.

Fatah, which began raising money, collecting weapons and training guerrilla fighters for raids into Israel, was one of more than a dozen such groups founded around the same time. But it was the earliest and largest of the bunch, which made it the most influential—and most troublesome to Arab governments, who regarded autonomous insurgent groups as both inconvenient and dangerous.

Hoping to rein in all these factions and channel their efforts to his own advantage, Egyptian President Gamal Abdel Nasser spon-

sored the creation of a new umbrella group in 1964: the Palestine Liberation Organization. To run it, Nasser hand-picked the Palestinian diplomat and lawyer Ahmed Shukairi.

Shukairi proved more adept at organizing conferences and issuing proclamations than raising an army, thus keeping a lid on the pressure cooker of Palestinian national aspirations until 1967. Then came the stunning Arab defeat in the Six-Day War, which drove several hundred thousand more Palestinians into the squalid exile of refugee camps, as Israel tore vast new swaths of territory from Arab hands. Palestinian fury erupted as never before. Within weeks, Shukairi was voted out as chairman of the P.L.O. and replaced with the leading advocate of aggressive armed struggle: Fatah chief Arafat.

Under Arafat, the P.L.O., then based in Jordan, embarked on a stepped-up program of cross-border raids into Israel. In 1968 the Israelis responded with an assault on the Jordanian town of Karameh, from which many of the raids had been launched. During the battle that followed, both sides were taken by surprise. Faced with the superior might of the Israeli army, the P.L.O. forces didn't behave like guerrillas and melt into the terrain. Instead, they stood their ground, faced the Israelis directly and fought tenaciously. Although neither side scored a decisive victory, the fact that the P.L.O. had met Israelis as equals on the battlefield did more to restore Palestinian pride and self-respect than any single event since 1948. To the wider world, Arafat was now the face of the Palestinian cause. ■

The Six-Day War

■ Surrounded on all sides by Arab armies, Israel gambles on a surprise attack and wins a sweeping victory that triples its size. But the new map of the region lays the groundwork for long years of bitterness

"THIS ACT WILL ASTOUND THE WORLD," BOASTED Egypt's leader, Gamal Abdel Nasser, on May 30, 1967, as his armies joined those of Jordan, Syria and Iraq in massing along the borders of Israel, preparing for an all-out assault. Nasser was right. But what stunned the world in the days that followed was not the long-promised extermination of Israel but rather the humiliating rout of the Arabs. In the Six-Day War that was launched by Israel on June 5, Israeli aircraft and armies thoroughly trounced Arab military forces, and the war ended with Israel taking control of enormous tracts of land from its neighbors.

Some of this new acreage, like the vast, arid spaces of the Sinai peninsula, was useless desert. Some, like the Golan Heights along Israel's border with Syria, was of crucial military significance. Some, like the Western Wall and al-Aqsa Mosque in the Old City of East Jerusalem, was of deep spiritual significance to Jews, Muslims and Christians. Yet all the lands occupied by Israel after the surprisingly brief conflict—as well as the hundreds of thousands of new Palestinian refugees the war created—would only exacerbate the region's tensions. For all these reasons, the Six-Day War is one of the most significant events in the recent history of the Middle East.

The roots of the war can be traced to Egypt, Syria and Israel. Eleven years after the Suez crisis, Nasser still aimed to be the great Arab leader who would remove Israel from the map. Syria's anger was much more specific: it was triggered by Israel's creation of the National Water Carrier, a huge irrigation project that would divert water from the Jordan River to nourish Israeli agriculture. Syria deeply opposed the plan, and throughout 1965 and 1966 Syrian soldiers rained artillery fire on Israeli settlers in the Hula Valley from the Golan Heights, 3,000 ft. above the valley. The skirmishing peaked on April 7, 1967, when Israeli planes shot down six Syrian jets, MiGs supplied by the Soviet Union.

Nasser now stepped in, mobilizing his troops to prepare for an invasion of Israel from the Sinai Peninsula. On May 16 he ordered the United Nations Emergency Force, in place since the Suez Crisis, to evacuate the region, and it did. Six days later, Nasser banned Israeli ships from the Straits of Tiran, Israel's crucial sea link to Asia and the oil fields of Iran.

As tensions mounted, King Hussein of Jordan—who was trapped between his U.S. allies, his fellow Arab leaders and his strongly pro-Nasser people—joined Egypt's alliance against Israel. Lebanon and Iraq followed suit. By May 30, when Nasser made his bold declaration, the Arabs claimed they had some 465,000 troops and 800 aircraft massed against Israel's 275,000 troops and 200 planes.

Israel's Prime Minister, Levi Eshkol, and his top military advisers decided they could not afford to wait for an attack and must instead strike the first blow. Early in the morning of

AFTERMATH: An Israeli tank rolls deep into the Sinai Desert, passing the body of a fallen Egyptian soldier. Egypt lost 15,000 men in the Sinai, while Israel lost only 800 on all fronts. At right, jubilant Israelis celebrate the capture of Jerusalem's Old City

June 5, all but 12 fighters of the Israeli air force flew out over the Mediterranean, then swung back to strike Egypt's airplanes on their air-fields. The surprise attack was devastating: within two hours, Egypt lost some 300 planes. When the Israeli jets returned, they were quickly serviced and sent back in the air to strike the air forces of Jordan and Syria, again wreaking havoc. Within the war's first hours, the tide was flowing in Israel's favor.

In the fierce ground battles that followed, Israel's control of the skies helped its forces prevail. In the Sinai Desert, Major General Ariel Sharon and his fast-moving tank corps whipped the Soviet-trained Egyptian armies, capturing the critical Egyptian town of Abu-Ageila in three days of battles. After it fell, Egypt's top commander ordered a general retreat, ensuring Israel's victory.

Jordan's King Hussein was loath to join the fight. But in the war's first hours, after Jordanian radar sighted planes flying from Egypt to Israel, Nasser lied, assuring Hussein that the planes were units of his air force, heading to strike Israel. Hussein quickly ordered his troops to begin shelling West Jerusalem. The planes, of course, were Israeli fighters returning from destroying Nasser's air force. Two days later, victorious Israeli troops entered the Old City in East Jerusalem, Judaism's holiest site. The Israelis also took control of the Gaza Strip and West Bank of the Jordan, and more than 300,000 Palestinians fled, creating a major refugee crisis in the region.

In the war's toughest battle, Israeli tanks launched a smashing uphill assault against heavily fortified Syrian positions in the Golan Heights, eventually driving the Syrian armies from the area. Finally, on June 10, Israel heeded calls from the U.S. and other concerned nations and accepted a cease-fire.

In six short days, the map of the Middle East had been redrawn. Most galling to Arabs, Israelis now were in control of the historic Old City of Jerusalem. Israel had won a great victory, but in their moment of triumph, Israelis had sown the seeds of future misery . ■

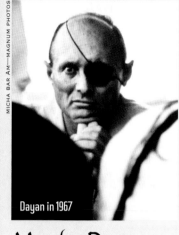

Dayan in 1967

Moshe Dayan

For millions around the world after the Six-Day War, its military hero Moshe Dayan was the living symbol of Israel, and no wonder: he was born the first child in the first Jewish kibbutz in Palestine, to Russian immigrant parents. Soldier, statesman and swashbuckling star of Israel's wars with its Arab neighbors, he was famed for his black eye patch (he lost his left eye on a 1941 reconnaissance mission in Syria) and round boyish face. Dayan occupied center stage in Israel for more than 30 years, and before his death in 1981, he had largely outgrown his image as a warrior and become an impassioned advocate of peace.

Dayan was a political maverick, immensely charming but fiercely independent and often gloomily distant. Fearless to the point of folly on the battlefield, he initiated the tradition of Israeli officers personally leading their troops into battle. To Dayan's credit, he came to appreciate the concerns of his adversaries more than most Israeli officials: he was sometimes disparaged by his colleagues as "that Arab." His conviction that Jew and Arab must learn to live together and his personal involvement in the post-1967 military occupation of the West Bank and Gaza Strip eventually made him a surprising advocate of a unilateral Israeli withdrawal from the lands he had helped win in 1967.

TORCHED: The burning of civilian jetliners in the Jordanian desert brought the militant Palestinian groups. to the world's attention. The U.S.S.R. urged its proxy, Syria, to assist the Palestinians, but Jordanian troops turned back Syria's forces. The U.S. and Israel supported the moderate Hussein

Jordan's Black September

■ Yasser Arafat and the P.L.O., acting in the name of Palestinian refugees, trigger a civil war inside Jordan—but King Hussein's troops send them packing

THIS IS JY-ONE," SAID THE AMMAN RADIO ANnouncer on Sept. 16, 1970. "Hussein on the mike." Seconds later, short-wave radio operators around the world became the first to hear what was happening inside Jordan, a nation that had been cut off from the outside world days earlier by a declaration of martial law. Acknowledging that a civil war had erupted in the streets, King Hussein said of the situation outside his palace, "We get a bit of blasting here ... it is a sad time. But we are putting our house in order and soon it will be organized."

Hussein's need to put his house in order had become apparent at the beginning of September, when militants from the Popular Front for the Liberation of Palestine (P.F.L.P.) hijacked three civilian airliners, taking hundreds of civilian hostages. Three of the jetliners were flown to a remote desert airstrip in Jordan, the fourth to Cairo; when negotiations for the hostages failed, the planes were blown up on live TV. Another planned hijacking failed. All the hostages ultimately escaped unharmed.

For Hussein, this signaled the opening of the last act in a drama that had been building to an uncertain conclusion for several years. A swelling population of Palestinian refugees, displaced from the country that had become Israel 22 years earlier, had reached the point of outnumbering the Bedouin tribesmen who thought of themselves as Jordanian citizens and regarded Hussein as their King.

Led by firebrand groups like Yasser Arafat's Fatah party and the P.L.F.P., the Palestinians set up a state within a state inside Jordan—complete with their own army. No longer willing to abide Hussein's cautious attempts to placate Arab nationalism without provoking Israeli retaliation, militant Palestinian leaders were determined to spark a war with Israel.

The September hijackings were only the most theatrical stunt in a succession of violent incidents that included years of cross-border raids into Israel, bombings and abductions. Within Jordan, Arafat's Fatah movement skirmished constantly with Hussein's police and army. The King narrowly survived several attempts on his life.

But this time the militants overplayed their hand. Hussein turned loose his seasoned Bedouin soldiers, along with hundreds of tanks and armored personnel carriers, against the rifles and hand grenades of the Palestinians — and the Syrian troops who invaded Jordan to support their cause. In less than two weeks, it was all but over: thousands of Palestinians, both fighters and civilians, lay dead or wounded; most Palestinians in Jordan were herded into refugee camps or expelled from the country. Among those who fled was Arafat, disguised as a Kuwaiti diplomat. By 1971 Arafat and the movement he led had found a new home: Lebanon. And their ouster from Jordan had been given a new name: "Black September."■

Terror at the Munich Olympics

■ Ruthless, anonymous and deeply committed, a new breed of terrorists takes Israeli athletes— and the rest of the civilized world—hostage to its cause in Germany

THE NAME "BLACK SEPTEMBER" BEGAN AS A BITTER reference to the date of the Palestinian Liberation Organization's military rout and expulsion from Jordan. Within months, however, the words had become a rallying cry and the name of a new terrorist group—an unacknowledged offshoot of Fatah, Yasser Arafat's P.L.O. faction—that sought to avenge this humiliation. The first attacks carried out by Black September were directed at Jordan. That country's Prime Minister, Wasfi Tal, was shot to death by four gunmen outside a Cairo hotel in November 1971. But Black September quickly graduated from assassination to massacre.

A few days before the second anniversary of the outbreak of fighting between Palestinian militants and the Jordanian govern-ment, eight men wearing sweatsuits scaled the fence of the lightly guarded Olympic Village in Munich, Germany, site of the 1972 Summer Games. Pulling AK-47s out of their athletic bags, they rounded up 11 Israeli athletes, coaches and a referee, shooting two dead in the first minutes of the attack. Before a global television audience of millions, the terrorists demanded the release of 234 prisoners from Israeli jails. Negotiations were ruled out by the Israelis, but the Germans began fake sessions to buy time. On the afternoon of Sept. 5, the Black September commander, distinctive in his white hat, insisted that his team and the hostages be flown to Cairo.

What followed was a ghastly fiasco. Two German helicopters choppered the captors and hostages to a military airfield. When Issa, as the Black September commander called himself, and a comrade inspected the Boeing 727 they had demanded for their getaway, it clearly wasn't ready to fly. As they raced back to the two helicopters, German snipers on the roof of a nearby building opened fire. The Palestinians shot out the lights on the tarmac, and the Germans were paralyzed for nearly an hour, until four armored police vehicles arrived. That prompted one terrorist to toss a grenade into one helicopter, and another to shoot the hostages in the other helicopter.

When the flames subsided, all the Israeli athletes were dead. Three Black September operatives survived; Germany freed them two months later in exchange for civilians taken hostage on a hijacked Lufthansa plane.

The Munich assault was designed to be spectacular, and by the terrorists' terms, it was a resounding success. Abu Iyad, the Arafat deputy who headed Black September, later explained that the hostage taking was meant "to use the unprecedented number of media outlets in one city to display the Palestinian struggle, for better or worse!" At Munich, Black September succeeded in making the Palestinian refugees' cause impossible to ignore, even as the world deplored the means with which the terrorists advanced it. This was terror on a new, grand, horrifying scale, perfectly calibrated for the Western media audience.

After Munich, for the first time, the larger world realized that, like the Israeli athletes, it was now being held hostage to the problems of the Middle East. As TIME observed with grim foresight in its Sept. 18, 1972, issue, terrorism was being "exported from the Middle East to the rest of the world, first to Western Europe, and maybe eventually even to the U.S." ■

HORROR: At Munich the world saw the new face of Middle Eastern terrorism: an anonymous man in a ski mask, holding innocent victims hostage to his demands and prepared to give his life for his cause

1972

1973

SHAKEN: Israel's Premier, Golda Meir, faced a debacle in the first hours of the Arabs' surprise attack

The Yom Kippur War

■ In the largest war fought in the Middle East in modern times, Egypt and Syria take Israel by surprise, but the shaken Israelis regroup to battle Arab armies to a standstill

OCTOBER 1973: ON THE SANDS OF THE SINAI Peninsula and the craggy hills of the Golan Heights, the smoldering carcasses of planes and tanks mingled with the rusting wreckage left over from the Six-Day War of 1967. Blackened bodies of slain troops littered the terrain. From Damascus to Cairo and over the neighboring countries of Lebanon and Jordan, dogfights swirled high in the sky, antiaircraft shells and missiles exploded, and debris fell to earth. On the ground, armies of Arabs and Israelis maneuvered and fought one another with an intensity never before witnessed in the seemingly endless conflicts of the modern Middle East.

The great war of 1973 violated the sacred calendars of two cultures: Jews call it the Yom Kippur War; to Arabs, it is the Ramadan War. As the conflict raged, TIME proposed a different name: the War of the Day of Judgment. By whatever name you call it, the conflict was a watershed event in Middle East history. It can fairly be seen as Act II of the Six-Day War of 1967, for it was launched by Egypt, Syria and neighboring Arab nations in order to regain control of the vast lands they had lost in that brief but boundary-altering conflict

At first it looked as if the Arabs would succeed. Only the timely intervention of the U.S. military in support of Israel prevented a possible annihilation of the Jewish state. Indeed

the war brought the world's two superpowers very close to a nuclear combat.

Early on, the man of the hour was Egypt's President, Anwar Sadat, long the butt of jokes for his repeated, hollow threats to regain the Sinai from Israel. But the two-front attack launched by Egypt and Syria on Oct. 6—Israel's holiest holiday, Yom Kippur—was well coordinated, and it was not until 10 hours before the attack that the Israelis realized it was coming. As Israeli soldiers scrambled from synagogues to put on uniforms, Syrian forces in the Golan Heights and Egyptian troops in the Sinai Peninsula, equipped with Soviet-supplied tanks, ground-to-air missiles and artillery, smashed through thinly manned Israeli lines and established powerful positions within the first minutes of the war.

Elation swept across Arab nations, many of which—including Lebanon, Iraq, Saudi Arabia, Kuwait, Libya, Algeria, Tunisia, Sudan and Morocco—had sent troops to fight Israel. Sadat was hailed, and even Jordan's King Hussein, at first content to stand by, dispatched his army into action. Israelis were rocked, shattered: both Premier Golda Meir and defense chief Moshe Dayan, hero of the Six-Day War, were castigated for their lack of preparedness.

Although Israeli troops took a beating in the war's first days, they rallied to stiffen their defense, sending most of their reserves to roll back the Syrian assault in the Golan Heights; on Oct. 10, Israeli fighters bombed the capital, Damascus. And Israeli troops managed to at least hold a line on the Egyptian front.

Deeply invested in the region, the world's two superpowers were soon drawn into the fray. As Soviet planes reinforced the Arab armies, U.S. President Richard Nixon decided to mount a massive airlift to resupply Israel. Most NATO powers, many of whom had economic interests in Arab nations, refused to take part. Only Portugal offered an airfield for refueling, and in the month between Oct. 14 and Nov. 14, 566 U.S. supply planes ferried 22,000 tons of matériel to Israel via Portugal.

The supplies were needed: in the greatest tank battle since World War II, the Israelis routed the Egyptians in the Sinai desert in mid-October. In a complete reversal of the war's beginning, both Damascus and Cairo were now threatened by Israeli forces. It was later revealed that the Soviet Union actively considered sending troops to the region at this moment; such an act might easily have escalated into a nuclear confrontation with the U.S. But both superpowers were loath to begin a war, and as U.S. Secretary of State Henry Kissinger applied pressure to the Israelis to accept a cease-fire, on both sides of the conflict the voices calling for peace outweighed those calling for further war .

As Kissinger began visiting the region's capitals in search of an accord, the frequent flyer was said to be practicing "shuttle diplomacy." He succeeded, brokering an agreement in which Israel returned control of parts of the Sinai to Egypt and U.N.-policed buffer zones were created between the adversaries, saving Sadat's reputation. Reaching an accord between Syria and Israel took longer, but a 1974 deal created a similar buffer zone, enforced by United Nations peacekeepers.

The shock of the war's early days took down Meir's government and savaged Dayan's legend. The hubris Israel had felt since the Six-Day War was now replaced by insecurity, even dread. On this Judgment Day, Israel's leaders were found wanting. ■

STIRRED: Israeli artillery rains shells on Syrian positions in the Golan Heights on Oct. 12, 1973

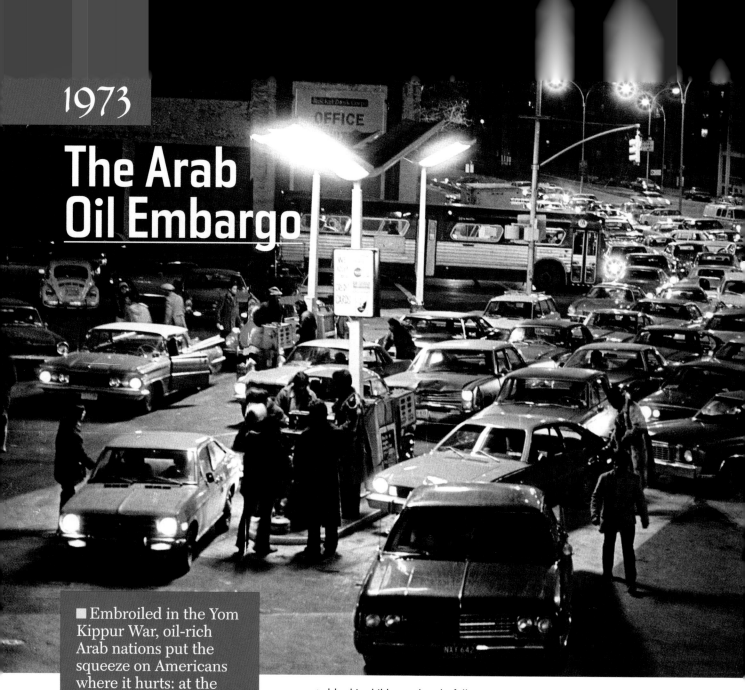

The Arab Oil Embargo

■ Embroiled in the Yom Kippur War, oil-rich Arab nations put the squeeze on Americans where it hurts: at the neighborhood gas pump

"RUSHING TO WORK LAST WEEK," TIME REPORTED in its Nov. 19, 1973, cover story about the Arab oil embargo that had begun a month earlier, "John Doe, American, swung his car onto the freeway—only to discover that the posted speed limit had been reduced from 60 m.p.h. to 50 m.p.h. When he stopped at a gas station for a refill, he learned that overnight the price had gone up 2¢ per gal. At his office he felt unusually cool because the thermostats had been pushed down a couple of degrees, to a brisk 68°. Later, when he finished work and was driving home, he noticed that the lights on outdoor advertising signs had been doused. In his living room he

was greeted by his children, who gleefully reported that their school would be closed for a month this winter—in order to save oil."

After years of muttering about using their abundant oil as a political weapon, newly unified Arab leaders unsheathed their devastating economic scimitar in mid-October. Enraged by their failure to overrun Israel after Egypt and Syria launched their surprise attack on Yom Kippur—and determined to punish the U.S. and Europe for their support of the Jewish state—OAPEC, the Organization of Arab Petroleum Exporting Countries, began to cut oil production, raising prices sharply. Experts predicted that the slowdown, which quickly escalated into a full-scale embargo, would lead to cold homes, hospitals and schools; shuttered factories; slower travel; brownouts;

consumer rationing; and runaway inflation.

Each of these predictions proved correct in the short run, but only the last of them lingered on: largely because of the oil crisis, the U.S. economy descended into a funk from which it would not emerge for nearly a decade. Yet coverage in many magazines and newspapers from the time echoes with a vaguely apocalyptic quality: for some, the death of the American Dream seemed to be at hand.

It's unfair, though, to blame commentators in 1973 for implying that the world was coming to an end. In a way, it was. The old order of limitless, inexpensive oil was passing away and being replaced by a new era, in which the price of Black Gold would rise and fall with demand, like any other commodity—regard-

STALLED: Motorists in Brooklyn, N.Y., line up to buy scarce gas on Dec. 23, 1973. Many in the line accused the station of price gouging: the owners were charging an unheard-of $1 for a gallon of gas

less of how much that inconvenienced the developed nations that bought it. And a new brand of political and economic respect would be commanded by the oil-rich nations that peddled the crude.

The crisis tested the close relationship between Saudi Arabia and the U.S. But the one lesson the oil embargo should have taught Americans—the cost of U.S. dependence on foreign energy sources—went unheeded. At the time the embargo was formally ended, in March 1974, "John Doe, American" was concerned about energy in a way that he never had been before. But when prices at the pump returned to their pre-embargo level, it proved all too easy to put America's need to develop alternative energy sources on the back burner of the national agenda. ◼

The King in 1969

King Faisal

Saudi King Faisal ibn Abdul Aziz al Saud was the architect of the new era ushered in by the Arab oil embargo of October 1973—and he was named TIME's Man of the Year for this naked show of economic power translated into political power. In his 11-year reign, Faisal ("Sword" in Arabic) presided over the first stages of the transformation of Saudi Arabia from a backward desert kingdom to a modern 20th century nation.

An absolute monarch of the kind not seen in the West since feudal times, Faisal was the benevolent paterfamilias to 3,000 Saudi princes and 2,000 royal women. That solid family and tribal base gave him enormous authority within his kingdom. Although he consulted senior princes and tribal chiefs on major issues, Faisal always reserved final decisions for himself. At a time when neighboring Arab states like Bahrain and Kuwait were experimenting with legislatures, he rejected calls for a Saudi parliament, seeing it as the crutch of a weak ruler.

In Arab tradition, however, an absolute monarch is, like the Pope, the servant of the servants of the Almighty. Even on the street, climbing into the front seat of his

Chrysler New Yorker, Faisal was apt to practice the noblesse oblige of the desert, pausing to listen to petitioners, some hardly more than beggars.

Leading the oil embargo against the West brought King Faisal widespread respect from leaders of the Arab world, many of whom had earlier scorned him as an unregenerate conservative: he shunned modern dress for the traditional long cotton lhawb that Arabs wear beneath an abayeh, or robe. But he also knew how to be lenient, slowly relaxing the stark strictures of Islam for his subjects—although never for himself. Faisal habitually prayed, as Islamic law commands, five times a day. When in Jidda, he liked to take a prayer rug to the shore and meditate beside the sea. On Thursday evenings, after visiting a mosque for prayers, he often invited other worshippers home with him for a postprayer repast.

That ability to balance tradition with tolerance augured well for Faisal's ability to navigate the treacherous shoals of modernizing his nation. But we'll never know how well the King would have handled that tricky transition. On March 25, 1975, he was assassinated by his half brother's son. Faisal was succeeded on the Saudi throne by one of his half brothers, Khalid.

1978

Breakthrough At Camp David

■ After fighting four wars in three decades, Israel and Egypt join hands under the guidance of a U.S. President, forging an enduring peace between their nations

FROM THE BEGINNING IT WAS A REMARKABLE meeting, a colloquy between the leaders of two nations that had waged a quartet of wars in 25 years and whose people had kept up a low-level guerrilla struggle during that time. Yet when U.S. President Jimmy Carter invited Egypt's President Anwar Sadat and Israel's Prime Minister Menachem Begin

to join him at the secluded presidential retreat, Camp David, in the Maryland mountains, it turned out, against all expectations, to be a summit of astonishing and ultimately historic achievement.

Recalling that event for this book, Carter hailed his fellow conferees, reserving extra praise for Sadat. "I don't think I ever had the complete trust of Begin," Carter said. "He was the most reluctant; the rest of the Israeli delegation were much more willing to make compromises."

But the White House deployed a convincing weapon, polling data, against Begin's objections. "Begin would say, 'My people will never accept this,'" Carter recalled, "but I could answer, truthfully and accurately, that a poll

taken the week before had indicated a majority of Israelis would support [the deal]."

After 13 days cloistered at Camp David, the three men returned to the White House on Sept. 17, 1978, to sign before TV cameras and the watching world two documents that were giant steps toward peace in the Middle East. The outcome was substantially more than anyone except perhaps Carter had believed possible before the summit began—and far more than any of the trio had anticipated right up to the day on which the summit was scheduled to end, apparently in failure.

That the summit didn't fail, even after Sadat and Begin had both announced their intention to leave, was primarily due to Carter, all of

Egypt and Israel, which had technically been at war since the latter's founding, in 1948, led to a formal peace treaty signed the following year. The second accord, an overall plan for regional peace between the Arab states and Israel, is today somewhat closer to being realized than it was in 1978, but only slightly.

In truth, Carter was not pleased with Israel's policies after the conference, saying today, "[They] violated the portion of the agreement that dealt with the Palestinians and the West Bank ... the Israelis announced that their reading of the agreement allowed them to continue building settlements in the occupied territories." In contrast, Carter today praises Sadat, describing him as "firm and courageous in his commitment."

Sadat returned the favor at the time; he was almost reverential in his praise of Carter for convening the meeting. "You took a gigantic step," he said, while Begin termed it "the Jimmy Carter conference." Indeed it was Sadat's startling 1977 decision to journey to Israel that had helped break new ground, but there was credit for all to share—and since they took that first giant step toward peace together, Egypt and Israel have never made war again. ∎

SMILE! They looked happy for the cameras, but Begin and Sadat avoided each other for much of the time they spent at the presidential retreat

Sadat in 1981

Anwar Sadat

His life was a skein of dualities. Long a bitter foe of the Jewish state, he became Israel's only friend in a hostile region. A self-styled defender of the Palestinians, he was cursed as a traitor to their cause. He preached the unity of Arab nations, but his policies shattered what fragile fraternity existed and isolated his country. A onetime revolutionary firebrand and a career military man, he died in a hail of bullets. Yet history remembers Egyptian President Anwar Sadat as a man of peace.

whose intellectual and moral strengths helped orchestrate a major piece of statecraft. After a clumsy beginning in Middle East policy, Carter willed himself to become an expert. By his second summer, he was. His vast appetite for detail paid off: he knew the West Bank and Jerusalem problems in depth, and he knew the larger implications of seemingly minute controversies.

Carter was tough when he needed to be, and he had the patience and stamina to outlast Begin and Sadat. As he reminded TIME, for 10 of the 13 days the men spent on the mountain, their mutual antagonism ran so deep they were communicating only through him.

The men returned with two agreements. The first, a framework for peace between

It was his search for peace that led Sadat in November 1977 to travel to Jerusalem and embrace his former enemies. Not only did Egypt's then leader of 7 years break a 29-year Arab ban on direct dealings with the Israelis, but he also went straight to the Knesset to proclaim his willingness "to live with you in permanent peace and justice." More than any other event since the birth of Israel in 1948, that courageous gesture transformed the political realities of a region bloodied and embittered by continual hate and violence. In a stroke, years of suspicion faded away.

Until Sadat's pilgrimage, no leader on either side of the Arab-Israeli blood feud had shown the courage and vision to seek a radical solution to the festering problem. His hosts were surprised, then exalted by his overture. So were tens of thousands of Egyptians, who greeted their smiling leader upon his return with chants of "Sadat! The man of peace."

Sadly for Egypt, and the Middle East, not everyone joined in blessing this peacemaker. Fanatics damned him; soon they would kill him.

GUILTY? A number of former U.S. hostages in Iran have charged that current Iranian President Mahmoud Ahmadinejad was a leader of the so-called students who held them. The captors at right in this photo bears a strong resemblance to Ahmadinejad, but the Iranians have strenuously denied that the former mayor of Tehran was involved in the hostage crisis

Iran Leads an Islamic Uprising

■ The dictatorship of Iran's pro-West Shah collapses, and the taking of 52 U.S. hostages heralds the dawn of extremist, militant Islam in the Middle East

FEW AMERICANS PAID HEED WHEN THEIR GOVERN-ment helped topple the regime of Iran's Mohammed Mossadegh in 1953: at the time, the Middle East and its concerns seemed far away, more the stuff of fable than reality. It took two events—the OPEC oil crisis of 1973 and the Iranian revolution and hostage crisis of 1979—to bring home to Americans the extent to which their nation was a stakeholder in the oil-rich Middle East.

The hostage crisis was Act II of an epochal event that is the founding moment of modern political Islamism; Act I was the religious-led revolution that overthrew the regime of Shah Reza Pahlavi and brought the long-exiled fundamentalist Shi'ite cleric Ayatullah Ruhollah Khomeini to power. (Ayatullah is an honorific reserved for senior mullahs.) Khomeini and his fellow conservatives resisted the secularist regime of the West-leaning Shah, whose SAVAC secret police force was notably brutal, whose modernizing tendencies offended Shi'ite fundamentalists, and whose economic success failed to improve the lives of Iran's masses. Khomeini went into exile in 1964 and helped keep up a drumbeat of revolution that finally found success in January 1979, when the ailing Shah and his wife fled the country.

On Feb. 1, 1979, the stern-faced Ayatullah, now 78, flew from Paris to Tehran, where he was greeted with adoration by the masses.

After only eight tumultuous days, as the nation's streets filled with fanatical followers of the Ayatullah, many bearing arms long stashed in mosques, Khomeini managed to wrest control of the nation from the Shah's appointed steward, Prime Minister Shahpour Bakhtiar. On Feb. 9, the Ayatullah went on the radio to announce, "The dictatorship has abandoned its last trench." The first Middle Eastern nation devoted to the cause of extremist Islam was now a reality.

The first fruits of the Islamists' victory came the following November, when radical supporters of the Ayatullah seized the U.S. embassy in Tehran, provoking a 444-day confrontation with the nation Khomeini called "the Great Satan." For Americans, the long days when their countrymen were held hostage by armed revolutionaries was a first, unsettling glimpse of the depth of the hatred many in the Middle East bore for the U.S.

After an ill-fated U.S. rescue mission went down in flames in the desert, Iran refused to release the hostages until after the end of Jimmy Carter's presidency. Muezzins of hatred, Iran's new rulers now cried their message of anti-Americanism across the Islamic world, and generations of terrorists would draw inspiration from their words and deeds. ■

ALAIN DEJEAN—SYGMA—CORBIS

The Ayatullah greets followers in 1979

Ayatullah Ruhollah Khomeini

He embodied everything the West found incomprehensible about the East: his intense, ascetic spirituality and air of otherworldly detachment; his medieval, theocratic mind-set, which drew its parallels and precedents from the Islamic world of the 7th century; the mystical certitude that he spoke in the name of Muslims everywhere. Iran's Ayatullah Khomeini translated his hatred of America into acts of terrorism and defiance that helped undermine the presidency of Jimmy Carter and led Ronald Reagan's Administration into the folly of the Iran-*contra* scandal.

Yet Khomeini had one foe—the Sunni-led Iraq of Saddam Hussein—whom he hated even more than the U.S., and in the 1980s he sent some 900,000 of his countrymen, many of them teenagers, into a futile and bloody eight-year war with their neighbors. Ironically, the man who despised the Shah's modern ways fueled the fires of rebellion against his regime with Western technology: during his 15 years in exile, he spread his message to his followers on smuggled audiocassette tapes.

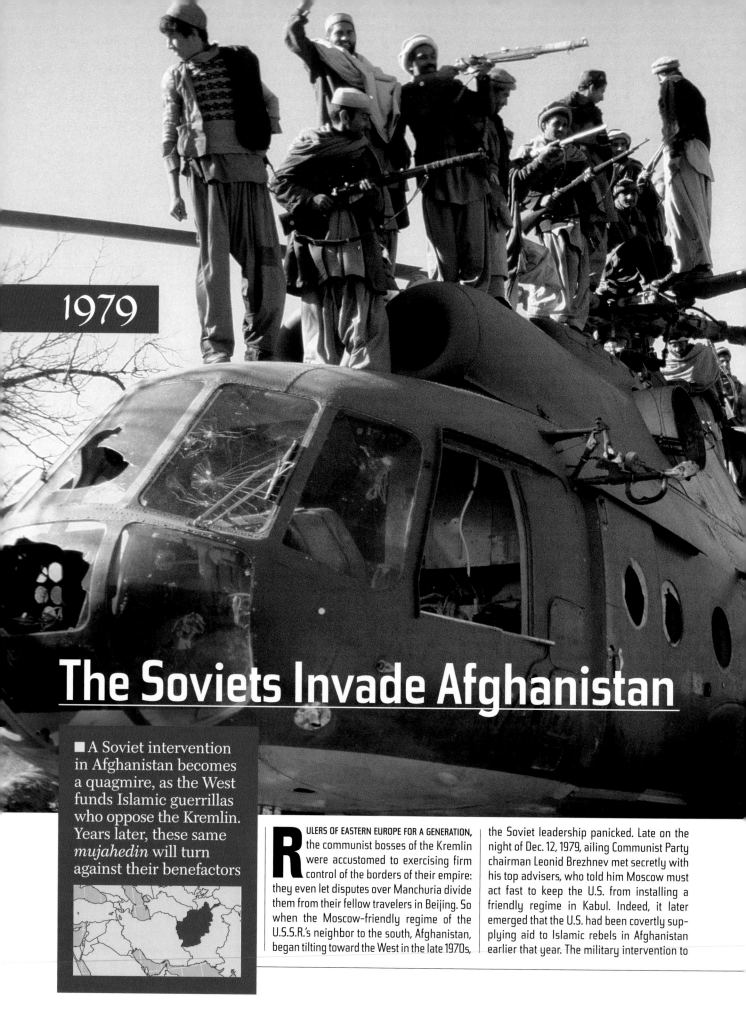

1979

The Soviets Invade Afghanistan

■ A Soviet intervention in Afghanistan becomes a quagmire, as the West funds Islamic guerrillas who oppose the Kremlin. Years later, these same *mujahedin* will turn against their benefactors

RULERS OF EASTERN EUROPE FOR A GENERATION, the communist bosses of the Kremlin were accustomed to exercising firm control of the borders of their empire: they even let disputes over Manchuria divide them from their fellow travelers in Beijing. So when the Moscow-friendly regime of the U.S.S.R.'s neighbor to the south, Afghanistan, began tilting toward the West in the late 1970s,

the Soviet leadership panicked. Late on the night of Dec. 12, 1979, ailing Communist Party chairman Leonid Brezhnev met secretly with his top advisers, who told him Moscow must act fast to keep the U.S. from installing a friendly regime in Kabul. Indeed, it later emerged that the U.S. had been covertly supplying aid to Islamic rebels in Afghanistan earlier that year. The military intervention to

TRIUMPH: Opposition to the Soviet intervention began early; here, *mujahedin* cheer their downing of a Soviet helicopter in January 1980

ALAIN DEJEAN—SYGMA—CORBIS

Vietnam. Throughout the 1980s Moscow poured troops and rubles into Afghanistan, yet they never managed to subdue the countryside, where tribal warlords held sway.

In this twilight era of the cold war, the U.S. embraced the enemies of the Soviets, the warlords and the Islamic guerrillas, or *mujahedin,* who rallied to their cause. As the U.S. would discover years later, the warlords of Afghanistan are a fractious lot, but the presence of a common enemy brought some of them together. Several groups of often hostile Afghans united to form the Seven-Party Alliance in 1980, working from Pakistan to defy Soviet rule.

Prodded by Republicans in Congress, in 1982 President Ronald Reagan committed $3.2 billion to Pakistan's President Mohammed Zia ul-Haq, much of which was funneled directly to the *mujahedin.* In 1985, when Soviet army helicopters posed the most severe threat to the *mujahedin,* the U.S. began supplying the rebels with Stinger surface-to-air missiles, further bedeviling the Soviets.

Yet the *mujahedin* were not simply anti-Soviet heroes: the struggle in Afghanistan helped create a new generation of Islamic jihadists. In one of history's great ironies, during the 1980s the U.S. made common cause with fanatical Islamic extremists like Osama bin Laden who would later turn their wrath on the U.S. and its Western allies.

By 1987 the U.S.S.R. was reeling from both its Afghan misadventure and the internal reforms launched by President Mikhail Gorbachev, and the Soviets began withdrawing from Afghanistan. By 1988 most Soviet troops had departed, after some 15,000 Soviet soldiers had died and billions of rubles had been spent in vain. They left behind 1 million dead Afghans and a nation that was not really a nation but rather a congeries of tribes and factions controlled by warlords like the Islamist Gulbauddin Hekmatyar and the pro-West Ahmed Shah Massoud.

It was Massoud who joined a fellow moderate warlord, Burhanuddin Rabbani, to found the Northern Alliance. In 1992 Massoud captured Kabul from the communist puppet who had survived the Soviet withdrawal, Najibullah. Four years later the capital fell again, this time to the extreme Islamists of the Taliban. With the Taliban in power and terrorists like bin Laden ensconced in Afghanistan, Massoud met the fate of so many Islamic moderates in recent years: he was assassinated by al-Qaeda on Sept. 10, 2001—the day before the 9/11 attacks: bin Laden and his cohorts were clearing the ground for the U.S. retaliation they expected in Afghanistan. ∎

put a Moscow-oriented government in place, Brezhnev was told, would be over in three or four weeks.

Two weeks later, Soviet soldiers already stationed in Kabul, augmented by air-lifted troops, pulled off the coup. Resistance was feeble: in a lightning series of events, Afghan President Hafizullah Amin was overthrown and executed, and Russian stooge Babrak Karmal was put into power. It was the most brutal blow from the Soviet Union's steel fist since the invasion of Czechoslovakia in 1968.

Yet if taking control of the government was simple for the Kremlin, taking control of the country proved impossible. As U.S. National Security Advisor Zbigniew Brzezinski predicted early on to President Jimmy Carter, the occupation of Afghanistan became the Soviets'

Iran and Iraq's 8-Year War

■ Their enmity fueled by religious infighting, Iran and Iraq engage in a bloody eight-year duel that bankrupts both nations, puts big-power alliances in play and sets the stage for further woe

AS AMERICANS WATCHED THE LONG, BLOODY WAR waged by Ayatullah Khomeini's Iran and Saddam Hussein's Iraq during much of the 1980s, they could be forgiven for invoking a quote from Shakespeare: "A plague on both your houses!" Still stinging from the Islamic revolution that had driven the pro-U.S. Shah from power in Iran—and had confined 52 of their countrymen for 444 days in Tehran—Americans shed no tears when Iraq's strongman, then only a year in power, sent his troops into Iran on Sept. 23, 1980.

As is so often the case in the Middle East, the war was spawned by an unstable amalgam of politics, piety and petroleum. The *casus belli* included Shi'ite-Sunni religious enmities dating back to the 7th century A.D., the control of the Khuzestan oil fields in western Iran and ongoing arguments over possession of the Shatt al-Arab waterway, a shipping lane formed by the confluence of the Tigris and Euphrates rivers along the southern border of the two nations. Iraq's major southern city, Basra, is located on the Shatt al-Arab, which is also home to Iraq's Marsh Arabs and is Iraq's only outlet to the Persian Gulf. Saddam regretted having ceded control of one-half the waterway to Iraq under the 1975 Algiers accord, and the water boundary in the middle of the strait remained the scene of frequent skirmishes between the two nations.

Taking a page from Israel's stunning surprise attack in the Six-Day War of 1967, Saddam launched the war by sending his French-built Mirage aircraft to destroy Iran's air force on the ground. The raid was a success, as were the ground invasions that followed, but after two years of steady Iraqi gains the

HENRI BUREAU—SYGMA—CORBIS

WASTED: An Iraqi soldier studies burning refineries bombed by his countrymen in Abadan, Iran in 1980

Iranians' resistance stiffened, and the war became a bloody stalemate. Even after Iraq withdrew most of its forces from Iran in 1982, Khomeini refused to sign a peace agreement, instead sending Iranian troops on the offensive into Iraq. In response, Saddam turned to the use of poison gas, a weapon long scorned and outlawed by the world community. By 1985 the combatants were routinely firing missiles and shells at each other's capitals.

Such major hostilities in one of the world's richest oil regions could not proceed in a vacuum. Israel did Iran a favor in 1981, bombing Iraq's nuclear reactor in Osirak. Many of Iran's arms were supplied by left-leaning regimes in Syria, Libya, North Korea and China. The world's two superpowers, still waging the cold war through proxies in Afghanistan, Central America and southern Africa, were also forced to take sides. The U.S.S.R. supplied many of Iraq's arms in the war's early years; Iraq also enjoyed the support of most Arab and many Western nations.

In 1985 U.S. President Ronald Reagan sent an envoy, Donald Rumsfeld, to visit Saddam and offer U.S. support to Iraq; considering later events, the picture of the two men smiling and shaking hands is a bracing reminder of the fleeting nature of global political alliances. Yet the Reagan Administration later found itself selling arms to Khomeini, under the illegal Iran-*contra* scheme hatched by White House loose cannon Oliver North.

As the war hobbled oil production in the region, attention focused on Iraq's ally Kuwait, and U.S. and European ships began protecting Kuwaiti oil tankers from Iranian ships and mines. When a Kuwaiti tanker hit an Iranian mine in 1987, support for Khomeini's cause withered, and he was forced to accept a United Nations–brokered cease-fire in July 1988.

At the war's end, both nations were nearly bankrupt, their oil fields were crippled and their armed forces were devastated. The overall death toll has been estimated at 1.5 million. The Shi'ite rulers of Iran had failed to wrest control of Iraq from Saddam's Sunni minority; Saddam had failed to take over the Khuzestan oil fields; and control of the Shatt al-Arab remained in dispute. Now, eager to get his hands on the rich oil fields to his south, Saddam began to study maps of Kuwait. ■

On the march against Iran, 1979

SIPA PRESS

Saddam Hussein

In the weeks before the Gulf War of 1991, the CIA presented George H.W. Bush with a psychological profile of Saddam Hussein. Iraq's strongman, it concluded, had a stable personality and was a rational, calculating decision maker. He did not suffer from mental illness. He was not exactly reckless, but he was comfortable wielding absolute power, using naked force and taking risks. He was wary and opportunistic and relied on only himself to make decisions. He ruled Iraq with an exquisite combination of terror and reward. And his sense of mission could taint his judgment.

Yet it was that sense of mission, his identification of himself with Iraq's destiny, that brought Saddam (Arabic for "He Who Confronts") to power in the first place. He was born just outside Tikrit, home of Saladin, Islam's great hero of the Crusades. Inspired by Egypt's Gamal Abdel Nasser, Saddam became a pan-Arabist and joined the Baathist Party. Exiled to Cairo after taking part in a failed 1959 coup, he returned to Iraq and helped lead the 1968 coup that brought his party to power. Oil revenues swelled in his days as Iraq's finance minister, and he rose to lead the party, which he purged in public in a terrifying July 1979 conference, initiating his long reign of terror over Iraq— during which his sense of mission clearly tainted his judgment.

1981

Israel Takes Out Saddam's Nukes

■ In a bold surprise attack, U.S.-built Israeli jets leave Saddam Hussein's nuclear dreams in ruins. But if a military success, the raid is a diplomatic setback for Menachem Begin

DURING THE FIRST HALF OF 1981, A SMALL GROUP of Israel's best air force pilots were ordered to a remote stretch of the Sinai desert. There, they began practice bombing runs against a full-scale model of a large, windowless concrete dome. Although kept in the dark about their target, the pilots recognized its distinctive shape as that of a nuclear power plant and deduced that their objective would be the Osirak facility, then under construction in Iraq.

Israel deeply feared an Iraq with nuclear weapons. As summer approached and the Iraqi reactor approached its start-up date, Israel's Prime Minister, Menachem Begin, weighed the options. The French government had designed the reactor and was building it for Saddam Hussein, but Begin's repeated entreaties to the

French to stop work had been ignored. Saddam insisted the reactor was intended for peaceful use, but few believed him. The facility could produce plutonium, bringing him one step closer to building nuclear weapons. Attacking it, though, would bring worldwide diplomatic protest, isolating Israel. And striking the facility after it was online would spread deadly radiation over a wide area of Iraq, killing thousands and inviting harsher condemnation.

On June 5, the 14th anniversary of the Six-Day War, Begin gave orders to launch an attack. Two days later, late in the afternoon of June 7, eight U.S.-built F-16 fighters took off from the Sinai desert. Accompanied by a fighter escort of six F-15s, they followed a zig-zag course designed to skirt radar installations in Saudi Arabia and Jordan (in whose airspace they trespassed), flying below 150 ft. to further avoid detection. By 5:10 p.m. Jerusalem time, the lead fighter penetrated Iraqi airspace, howling through the Sunday twilight at 400 m.p.h. Fifty minutes after takeoff, the warplanes sighted their target, the reactor's distinctive containment dome.

The lead F-16 fired a pair of video-guided smart bombs to punch through predetermined spots in the domed concrete. The following aircraft launched their own explosives through the jagged holes: a dozen conventional bombs weighing 2,200 lbs. each. After a

DOOMED DOME: The Osirak reactor in Iraq, as it appeared prior to Israel's pre-emptive attack

series of shattering roars, the roof collapsed, burying the reactor's radioactive core under hundreds of tons of concrete and steel debris. Fire raged through the site. Then the jets streaked for home, leaving behind 11 dead (10 dead Iraqi soldiers, one French technician) and the mangled nuclear ambitions of Iraq.

The backlash Begin had expected was not long in coming but was more serious than he anticipated: even the U.S. joined in voting for a U.N. Security Council resolution condemning the attack. Within Israel, cynics pointed out that Begin, in the midst of a tight race for re-election, received a huge boost from the raid. He won the race three weeks later.

If Israel's surprise attack was widely condemned at the time, it has come to be regarded by many as a successful setback to Saddam's growing threat. Ten years later, during Operation Desert Storm, the U.S. and the global coalition that fought Saddam's invasion of Kuwait had reason to be thankful that the Scud missiles Iraq fired into Israel and Saudi Arabia did not carry nuclear warheads. In 2006, as President Mahmoud Ahmadinejad continued to insist Iran would pursue nuclear capabilities, the White House was reported to be actively studying a pre-emptive strike on Iran similar to Israel's 1981 attack on Iraq. ■

Sadat Assassinated

■ Anwar Sadat, a great force for peace and moderation in the Middle East, is gunned down by militants invested in disorder

AS EGYPT'S PRESIDENT ANWAR SADAT BASKED IN international acclaim for his epochal decision to make peace with Israel, his domestic opponents grew more embittered and enraged. Egyptian militants like those in the fanatical Islamic Jihad terror group believed that Sadat must die: the man who saw peace as his "sacred mission" was in the crosshairs of those who believed just as strongly that they were doing God's bidding.

By the fall of 1981, the Nobel laureate, however idolized by the Western world, realized that dissidents at home were a problem. He ordered more than 1,000 arrests of suspected rebels in September alone, but he believed that his security forces had the situation in hand.

So when Sadat donned his gold-braided field marshal's uniform to review a military parade on Oct. 6, he saw little reason for concern. The occasion was Egypt's annual celebration of its own military might: perversely, it was also the anniversary of the 1973 surprise attack on Israel that triggered the Yom Kippur War in which Egypt was routed.

Earlier in 1981, Egyptian cleric Sheik Omar Abdel Rahman (who would later be convicted for planning a terrorist bombing spree in the U.S.) had issued a fatwa calling for Sadat's death. Rahman's followers within the Egyptian army saw the parade as their chance to carry out his ruling.

As a squadron of air force jets flew overhead, a truck stopped in front of the President's reviewing stand, and Sadat stood to receive a salute. He was greeted instead with a fusillade of automatic weapons fire, followed by several hand grenades, as a squad of mutinous soldiers emerged from the back of the truck. The reviewing stand was transformed into a *Guernica* of tumbled chairs and bodies smeared with blood. Sadat and six others were fatally wounded. The man who often answered warnings with the words, "This is my fate; I have accepted my fate" died within an hour. As his enemies had hoped, the death of this visionary dealt a crippling blow to the cause of moderation in the Middle East. ■

Defendant 113 in 1981

Ayman al-Zawahiri

Among the hundreds of Egyptians arrested in the wake of Sadat's assassination was Ayman al-Zawahiri, a surgeon known to be a member of Islamic Jihad, the militant group responsible for the assassination. Released for lack of evidence implicating him directly in the deed, "Defendant 113" left Egypt in the mid-1980s and went to Afghanistan. Fighting there against Soviet troops, he formed an alliance with another jihadist, Osama bin Laden. By 1995, after dispatching a squad of suicide bombers to the Egyptian embassy in Pakistan (where they killed 15 people), al-Zawahiri was back in Egypt, where authorities believe he engineered a failed attempt on the life of Sadat's successor, Hosni Mubarak.

Going underground, al-Zawahiri remained in Egypt and is credited with planning the 1997 massacre of more than 60 foreign tourists at the Luxor archaeological site. In 1999, for both these crimes, he was sentenced to death in absentia by an Egyptian court. He is also believed to have played a major role in planning the deadly 1998 attacks on U.S. embassies in Africa, which killed more than 200 people. That same year, he returned to Afghanistan and merged Islamic Jihad, which he had risen to lead, into bin Laden's expanding terrorist group, al-Qaeda.

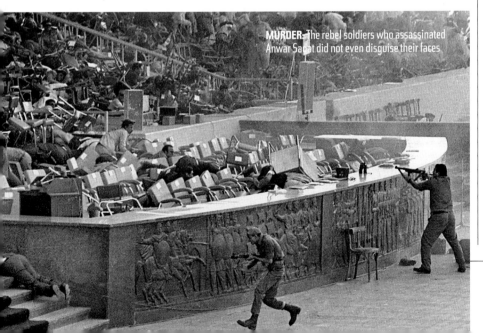

MURDER: The rebel soldiers who assassinated Anwar Sadat did not even disguise their faces

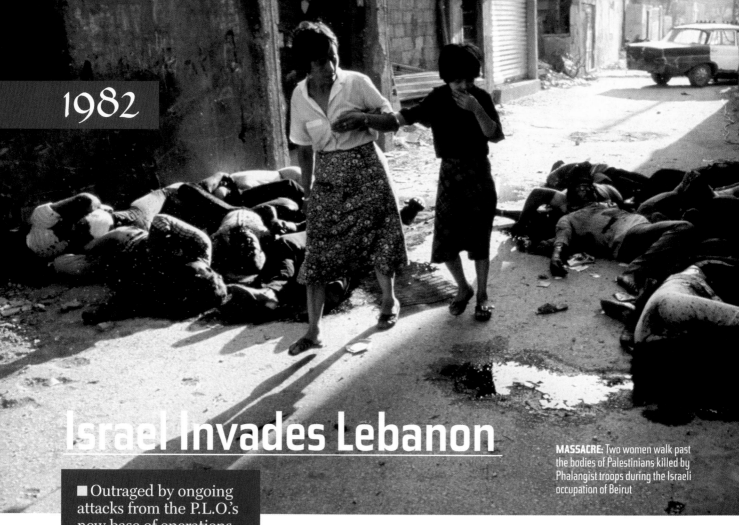

Israel Invades Lebanon

MASSACRE: Two women walk past the bodies of Palestinians killed by Phalangist troops during the Israeli occupation of Beirut

■ Outraged by ongoing attacks from the P.L.O.'s new base of operations, Israel sends troops into Lebanon and puts the militants to flight—but a massacre of Palestinians mars Israel's reputation

PEACE IN THE MIDDLE EAST, THIN AS AN EGGSHELL at the best of times, can be shattered into shards by the most arbitrary of causes—such as the June 1982 shooting of Israel's ambassador to Britain, Shlomo Argov, by a Palestinian militant. Although intelligence indicated that the attack was not the work of the P.L.O., that spark touched off Israel's long-simmering frustration at more than a decade of cross-border raids and missile attacks by the P.L.O. from Lebanon, where it had been stationed since being driven out of Jordan 12 years earlier.

Israel responded with two days of punishing air, land and sea raids on P.L.O. strongholds in Lebanon, after which Israeli tanks and troops poured over the Lebanese border in a three-pronged invasion along a 33-mile front. Meeting little resistance, Israel's defense chief Ariel Sharon exceeded the authorization given to him by Prime Minister Menachem Begin, which envisioned creating only a buffer zone in southern Lebanon, and drove his troops all the way to the outskirts of the capital, Beirut.

Although many of the P.L.O.'s fixed positions and much of its long-range Soviet-built artillery had been eliminated from southern Lebanon early in the fray, the Israelis continued to push northward, encountering Syrian troops who had been stationed in northern Lebanon's Bekaa Valley since 1976. Initial skirmishes with Syrian soldiers quickly gave way to outright battles, including aerial dogfights, raising the possibility of a wider regional war. In the meantime, Israel's forces surrounded Beirut and pounded much of the city into rubble.

Many Israelis who had supported the country's earlier wars based on clear threats to national survival now feared that a measured response to repeated provocation had spilled over into military adventurism. The questions mounted in tandem with the death toll: more than 600 Israeli soldiers would die in Lebanon.

The nagging doubts soon metastasized into outrage. On Sept. 16, soldiers of the Phalangists, a Lebanese Christian militia closely allied with the Israelis, entered two Palestinian refugee camps, Sabra and Shatila, with the consent of Israeli forces. Their target: P.L.O. fighters hiding in the camps. But furious at the recent assassination of Lebanon's newly elected Christian President, Bashir Gemayel, they spent the next 12 hours methodically executing as many as 800 unarmed civilians, including women and children. The massacres severely damaged Israel's reputation, even with close allies like the U.S.

Goaded by the Reagan Administration to stop the bloodshed, Israel agreed to a ceasefire that allowed Arafat and the P.L.O. to abandon their positions in Beirut. (In a replay of its 1970 expulsion from Jordan, the P.L.O. would now make its home in Tunisia.) In addition, Israel began a gradual withdrawal to a security zone in southern Lebanon, the original objective of the operation. Here, Israel's troops would remain until 2000, when the Israelis deemed the region pacified. The uneasy peace that followed lasted until 2006, when the abduction of two Jewish soldiers by the terrorist group Hizballah sent Israeli soldiers rolling into Lebanon once again. ■

The U.S. Barracks Bombing

■ U.S. troops on a peacekeeping mission in Lebanon are sitting ducks for a new tactic—suicide bombing—as practiced by members of a new terrorist organization: Hizballah

LATER, A MARINE SENTRY WHOM THE DRIVER BAR-reled past would remember only one thing: "He was smiling." On guard outside a military barracks at the Beirut airport, the sentry was powerless to stop the speeding truck, for the U.S. troops in Lebanon were required to stand guard duty without any ammunition in their rifles. That, along with the absence of road blocks, gave the driver a clear approach to his target: the barracks where hundreds of U.S. Marines were sleeping in the early-morning hours of Oct. 23, 1983.

The Marines were part of an 1,800-strong contingent of U.S. troops that had been sent to Lebanon in the autumn of 1982. Along with French, Italian and British troops, they made up the Multinational Force in Lebanon, which had been deployed to supervise the evacuation of the P.L.O. from that country, cover the withdrawal of Israeli troops (who had been fighting in Lebanon since the previous summer) and stabilize a situation that was spiraling into a full-scale civil war. The first two missions were accomplished in short order. The third proved impossible.

As the truck smashed through the front doors of the airport's Aviation Safety Building (which served as the field headquarters of the Eighth Marine Battalion), a blinding flash was followed by a deafening roar. The truck was packed with more than a ton of high explosives. In an instant, 241 U.S. servicemen were killed or mortally wounded, making it the bloodiest day for the Marine Corps since the World War II landing on Iwo Jima.

At almost the same moment, two miles away, another truck laden with explosives crashed into a building used by French paratroopers, killing more than 50 troops assigned to the Multinational Force. As surviving U.S. and French soldiers worked feverishly to free comrades trapped in the rubble, they were set upon by snipers.

Ghastly as the attacks were, their full import was not entirely apparent at the time: they were the first significant, modern instance of suicide bombing, as well as the first application of a new tactic: simultaneous, coordinated terrorist bombings. The two explosions also marked the debut of a new militant group (backed by Iran and Syria) that was previously unknown, but from whom much would be heard in the future: Hizballah. ■

SURVIVOR: Marines struggle to free a fellow soldier from the rubble of the U.S. barracks at the Beirut airport

1986

The U.S. Bombs Libya

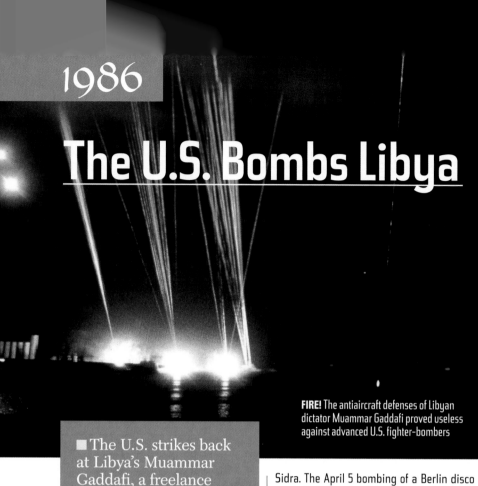

FIRE! The antiaircraft defenses of Libyan dictator Muammar Gaddafi proved useless against advanced U.S. fighter-bombers

Libya's strongman in 1986

■ The U.S. strikes back at Libya's Muammar Gaddafi, a freelance bankroller of terrorism

ON APRIL 14, 1986, U.S. PRESIDENT RONALD REAgan sent 33 U.S. fighters and bomber jets roaring toward five targets in Libya. The goal: to punish Libyan dictator Muammar Gaddafi, the man Reagan had taken to calling the "mad dog of the Middle East." The outcome was far from perfect: the U.S. lost a jet and its two-man crew and caused some civilian casualties and damage—including the death of Gaddafi's adopted 15-month-old daughter Hanna.

Plans for a strike of some sort against Libya began late in March when U.S. intelligence learned that Gaddafi intended to continue bankrolling terrorist acts, like the December 1985 strikes against the Rome and Vienna airports that killed 18 people. The attack came after months of escalating tension in 1986, including a March dogfight between U.S. Navy and Libyan jets over the contested Gulf of Sidra. The April 5 bombing of a Berlin disco made the U.S. strike all but inevitable.

Gaddafi's furious quest for revenge would yield a deadly harvest: within weeks, three British and American hostages held in Lebanon were hanged by their Libyan-supported captors; a British journalist was kidnapped in Beirut (and held for five years); and a U.S. scholar was shot dead in Jerusalem. The outrages peaked in 1988, when Libyan terrorists planted bombs aboard Pan Am Flight 103, bound for New York City. It exploded in the skies over Lockerbie, Scotland, killing 270 people.

Yet in a stunning turnabout, Libya's tiger has changed his stripes in recent years, abandoning decades of provocation and inviting international arms inspectors to dismantle his country's nuclear weapons program.

While Gaddafi indicates that geopolitical shifts like the collapse of the Soviet Union, the Palestinian decision to negotiate with Israel and the increasing spread of Islamic extremism forced him to change course, he also told TIME in 2006 that it was his atom bomb program that enabled him to deal with the West from a position of strength. Both the U.S. and Britain restored diplomatic relations with his nation, and as of 2006, Libya seems intent on hewing to its surprising new course as a law-abiding member of the world community. ■

Muammar Gaddafi

Even fellow Arab chieftans are baffled by Libya's leader: Egypt's Anwar Sadat called him "a mental case" and "a lunatic." But the square-jawed colonel is beloved in the country he has led since he presided over the 1969 army coup that deposed 80-year-old King Idris. Gaddafi, then only 27, soon began to apply his peculiar brand of Arab nationalism to his country, closing down U.S. and British military bases, expelling 25,000 descendants of Italian colonials, nationalizing foreign banks and imposing Shari'a.

Delighting in his role as outlaw, in the 1980s the Nasser wannabe and longtime Soviet client bankrolled the Black September terrorists, dispatched "death squads" to Europe and the U.S. to murder Libyans opposed to his rule and proffered arms and money to leftist "liberation" movements across the globe, from the Irish Republican Army to Muslim rebels in the Philippines.

Gaddafi flies by the seat of his pants, defying expectations. Coming in from the cold after long years as an outcast, this former enemy of the West has in recent years reached out to open the door to the international community, even abandoning his fledgling nuclear program. In a region generally tilting toward militant extremism, Libya's sudden swerve to the center is perfectly in character for that perennial loose cannon, Gaddafi the gadfly.

The Palestinian *Intifadeh*

■ Rebelling after long years of exile and neglect by their fellow Arabs, Palestinians stage a cut-rate revolt, defying Israel's domination

THE WORD TRANSLATES AS "UPRISING," AND IN THIS case the name rings true: the *intifadeh* that began in the Palestinian territories occupied and administered by Israel swelled up from the lowest ranks of the Arab world's outcasts in the last days of 1987. Frustrated as much by the corruption and in-competence of their own leaders as by Israel's continued occupation, young Palestinians also felt abandoned by foreign Arab governments, who toned down their anti-Israeli bombast in the mid-1980s as they cultivated increasingly close relations with Washington. So the upstarts rejected the top-down use of violence favored by established resistance groups like the P.L.O. and simply took to the streets. "Who's running the insurrection?" TIME asked rhetorically in a May 9, 1988, story. Answer: "As the Israelis—and P.L.O. Chairman Yasser Arafat—should know by now, the *intifadeh* seems to be run-ning itself."

At first, the uprising was the work of angry young men, known locally as the *shabab* (loose translation: "guys"), driven by the bitter frustration of two decades of Israeli rule. Years of accumulated grudges and humiliations—nurtured by Israeli assassinations of militant leaders, mass arrests of protesters and the demolition of homes belonging to family members of suicide bombers, among other measures—erupted in a series of riots in De-cember 1987. Soon middle-class shopkeepers, poor villagers and refugees in the occupied territories followed the *shabab* and picked up the only weapons at their disposal—rocks and clubs—and began the first widespread, grass-roots resistance to Israeli rule.

Cleverly positioning themselves as Arab Davids against an Israeli Goliath, the *shabab* confronted Israeli troops directly, daring them to shoot. When at first the troops did so, it only fed the flames of *intifadeh* and brought a surge of sympathy for the Palestinian cause.

The *intifadeh* gave birth to a diffuse and decentralized underground of local popular committees and anonymous coordinators that survived both the targeted killing of several leaders and the arrest of nearly 5,000 sup-porters in the revolt's first months. By 1990, the uprising had directed world attention and sympathy to the plight of the Palestinians in a way that murderous terrorist groups never did. The resulting pressures led to the 1991 Madrid Conference, the beginning of Israel's dialogue with Palestinian representatives. ■

ROCK OF RAGES: The sight of frustrated youths fighting Israeli occupation with sticks and stones helped sway world opinion to the Palestinian cause

ERIC FEFERBERG—AFP—GETTY IMAGES

SLAIN: A mother clasps her child in death in the city of Halabja, site of the single most deadly gas attack. Said one photographer: "It was like life frozen"

1988

Saddam Attacks the Kurds

■ Saddam Hussein earns the world's scorn when he deploys deadly nerve gas against his own citizens, the Kurds of northern Iraq

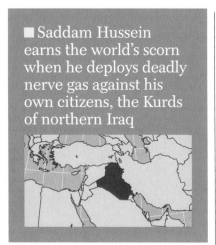

AFTER CONSOLIDATING HIS GRIP ON POWER IN Iraq in 1979, strongman Saddam Hussein demonstrated time and again that he was utterly ruthless in rooting out perceived enemies and removing any obstacle that stood in the way of his vision for Iraq. In the late 1980s, one such obstacle—the approximately 5 million ethnic Kurds living in the north of Iraq, near the border with Iran—was giving the Iraqi dictator fits. The Kurds, bitter enemies of Saddam, were aiding the Iranians in the long, seesaw war Iran and Iraq fought throughout the 1980s.

Saddam decided to act, and he chose as his agent of destruction his cousin Ali Hassan al-Majid, head of the Northern Bureau of the ruling Baath Party. After Saddam put al-Majid in control of the region in 1987, the new boss quickly declared specific areas of the Kurdish region "prohibited zones"—off-limits to the Kurds who had lived there for generations.

Saddam deployed an arsenal of cruel tactics to extinguish the Kurds: aerial bombardments, systematic destruction of towns, firing squads, torture. Some Kurds fled to rebel strongholds in the mountains of the region; many more starved or lived outside Iraqi towns as beggars. Some were shipped off to squalid camps in the nation's south; others were imprisoned under appalling conditions.

Yet such measures weren't enough to satisfy Saddam. In what came to be known as the al-Anfal campaign, al-Majid oversaw the execution of some 182,000 Kurds. Along the way, Saddam earned a dubious distinction, joining Adolf Hitler in using poison gas as a weapon of extermination against his own citizens, while al-Majid earned the nickname he has had ever since: "Chemical Ali."

Al-Majid dropped both mustard gas and the nerve gas sarin on rebel areas beginning in 1987. In the most notorious incident, which was technically not part of the al-Anfal campaign, a variety of nerve gases was dropped on the village of Halabja, then held by Iranian troops, from March 16 to 19, 1988, killing an estimated 5,000 civilians.

Saddam called this ghastly exercise in ethnic cleansing "Arabization," saying his goal was to eliminate non-Arab elements from Iraqi culture. The World Court at the Hague later used a more apt term to describe it: genocide. In one welcome outcome of the U.S. incursion into Iraq, on Aug. 21, 2006, 18 years after the events at Halabja, both Saddam and al-Majid were hauled into a Baghdad courtroom and formally charged with the mass murder of thousands of Kurds. ■

Bin Laden Becomes Jihad's Boss

THE EXPLOSION WAS SO LOUD IT WAS HEARD several miles away, and its reverberations would eventually travel around the globe. The car was nearing its destination, the al-Falah Mosque in the Pakistani frontier city of Peshawar, when it hit the land mine. All four passengers in the vehicle—a father with his two young sons and another youth—were killed.

Chief among the dead that Friday, Nov. 24,

■ A leader of the *mujahedin* fighting the Soviet occupation of Afghanistan is killed, and a well-educated Saudi aristocrat becomes the world's foremost jihadist

1989, was Sheik Abdullah Azzam, 48. It was the second attempt on his life. Earlier that year, a bomb had been planted beneath the pulpit of a mosque where he was supposed to preach and pray, but it hadn't exploded. Azzam, a Palestinian, had become the most prominent advocate of a jihad to save the Muslim lands from "infidel" encroachment. Thanks in part to his writings and diatribes, Islamic fighters from around the world, the *mujahedin,* traveled to Afghanistan to defeat the Soviet Union.

Azzam's killers have never been identified. But the man who gained the most from his demise was his deputy, Osama bin Laden, who took over the role of first among the jihadists. Bin Laden, a wealthy, Riyadh-born Saudi, had attended the secular al-Thager Model School in Jidda; as a student at King Abdulaziz University there, he first came into contact with the Islamist teachings of Egypt's Muslim Brotherhood—and with Azzam. He followed Azzam to Afghanistan in the early 1980s,

where the two men operated the Maktab al Khidmat (Office of Order), which funneled money and arms to the *mujahedin;* bin Laden served as its chief financier.

Disagreement between master and protégé over the shape of a post-Soviet Afghanistan led to a parting of ways in early 1989, and soon bin Laden went off to found al-Qaeda. With Azzam dead, bin Laden assumed ideological seniority in the movement.

Following the Soviet withdrawal from Afghanistan, bin Laden returned to the Middle East, where he grew increasingly frustrated by the U.S. presence in his homeland, which reached a peak in the Gulf War of 1991. After operating out of Khartoum, Sudan's capital, for several years, bin Laden was expelled from the nation; he returned to Afghanistan to establish training camps for a new generation of jihadists—and to expand his struggle from the Islamic Middle East deep into the heart of the "infidel" West. ■

GUERRILLA: Few photos of bin Laden were taken during his days battling the Soviet takeover of Afghanistan; this picture from 1988 is one of them

1991

Operation Desert Storm

■ Forging a strong coalition of surprising allies that heralds a new age in the Middle East, President George H.W. Bush rolls back Saddam Hussein's takeover of neighboring Kuwait

AT THE END OF THE 1980S, IRAQ AND IRAN WERE emerging from a long, inconclusive war that had served only to kill or maim millions of their citizens and bankrupt their treasuries. But Saddam Hussein's apparent need to find enemies to fight was not sated: now he directed his ire to the south, where the oil-rich nation of Kuwait was disrupting Iraq's economy. Iraqis already regarded Kuwait's mere existence as an error; they saw it as a province of Iraq unlawfully detached by the British after World War I, much as the People's Republic of China views Taiwan. Iraq owed deep debts to Kuwait from funds borrowed during its war with Iran, and Saddam also believed Kuwait was drilling "slant wells" under the border to steal Iraqi oil.

On Aug. 2, 1990, Saddam sent Iraqi troops rolling into his tiny neighbor to the south; within 24 hours the Emir had fled, and Iraqis were in control. Here was a naked power grab seldom seen since Hitler's late-1930s heyday. Ominously, Saddam also had his eye on Saudi Arabia's oil fields to the west; thousands of his troops set up camp along the border.

Soon the lines between Riyadh and Washington were humming, and on Aug. 7 the Saudis officially requested U.S. aid against Iraq's threat. The U.S. Navy quickly began a blockade of Iraq's oil-exporting ports, and the Pentagon launched Operation Desert Shield, sending 230,000 U.S. troops, including 35,000 women, to Saudi Arabia.

Alert to Arab and global opinion, Bush and his chief ally (and spine stiffener), British Prime Minister Margaret Thatcher, decided to enlist a broad coalition of allies to fight Saddam. The alliance they created was a clear signal that with the fall of the Berlin Wall in 1989, a new age had dawned in which longtime cold war rivalries no longer held sway. Bush called it a new world order: marching with Uncle Sam in the anti-Saddam coalition were not only the NATO countries and Japan but also such unlikely bedfellows as Syria, Egypt, Afghanistan, Morocco and Pakistan; even the Soviets lent their support. Israel did not join the coalition owing to Arab sensitivities; Jordan, with close economic ties to Iraq, remained neutral. The P.L.O. supported Iraq.

The allies issued an ultimatum to Saddam: Withdraw from Kuwait by Jan. 15, 1991, or face the consequences. Saddam didn't budge. On the evening of Jan. 16, viewers in the U.S. and around the world turned on their TVs to see a war begin in real time, as U.S. and British planes fought their way through antiaircraft fire to pound Baghdad.

Yet Iraqis withstood the aerial onslaught and aimed their wrath precisely where the world expected them to: at the scapegoat nation of Israel. Saddam fired 42 Soviet-designed Scud missiles into Israel, where the tough Israelis hunkered down and, at Bush's urging, bravely refrained from fighting back. Saddam fired Scuds into Saudi Arabia as well; one missile killed 28 U.S. troops in Dhahran.

The war's ground campaign, marshaled by the highly capable U.S. General Norman Schwarzkopf, was launched Feb. 24. Although Saddam had promised his countrymen "the mother of all battles," the fight was a mismatch. Following an initial feint from Saudi Arabia into Kuwait, Schwarzkopf hurled the full brunt of his attack directly into Iraq, taking the Iraqis completely by surprise. They were routed, and within only 100 hours of its commencement, the ground war was halted, as coalition troops took control of Kuwait City after mowing down retreating Iraqi soldiers along the main highway leading from Kuwait to Iraq. On their way out, the Iraqis left a final, despicable calling card, putting the torch to thousands of Kuwaiti oil wells and creating a months-long environmental calamity.

Yet if Operation Desert Storm was a triumph of diplomacy and warcraft, its conclusion was unsatisfying. Bush and the allies decided not to unseat Saddam, fearing that an Allied occupation of Iraq might become a quagmire. That decision, widely criticized at the time, has been regarded with new respect after the 2003 incursion into Iraq left U.S. troops fighting just the sort of ongoing sectarian battles U.S. strategists feared in 1991.

Instead, in a tragedy that could have been avoided, the allies urged two of Iraq's restless minorities, the northern Kurds and southern Shi'ites, to rise up, in the hope that Saddam might be brought down from within. Instead, the dictator took revenge upon the two groups, ruthlessly squashing both rebellions at a cost of thousands of lives, while the Allies stood by, refusing to intervene.

Saddest of all, the new world order Bush hoped to nourish never took root. The Gulf War coalition was a one-off: its promise that Syria and the U.S. might find common cause would prove to be a brief, shining illusion, a mirage of peace shimmering in a hot desert wind. ∎

ENDGAME: U.S. troops prowl for retreating Iraqi soldiers, who set wells in the Burgan oil fields in southeast Kuwait ablaze as they left the country. At its peak, the number of U.S. soldiers in the region during Desert Storm reached 380,000

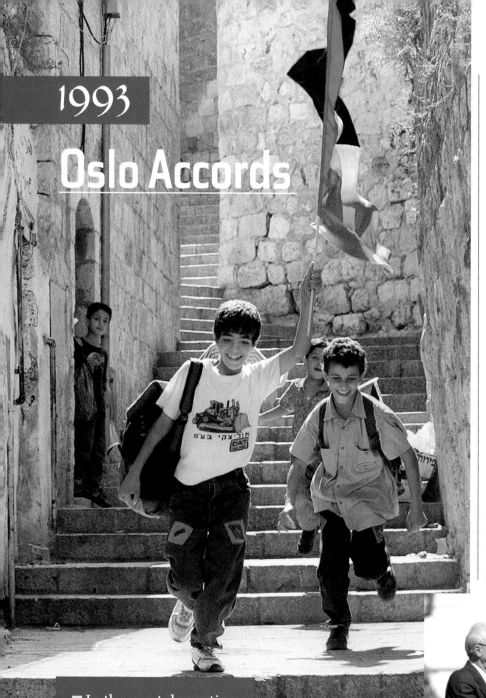

1993

Oslo Accords

signed by the peacemakers, was the affirmation of a new era in which its witnesses could believe, an era thrust upon an unsuspecting world with stunning swiftness. The parchment they signed was a framework for interim Palestinian self-government, as well as a document meant to bind Israel and the Palestine Liberation Organization to further constructive deliberation.

The handshake was the culmination of months of secret negotiations between emissaries of the Israeli Prime Minister and the chairman of the P.L.O. Ironically, it was the product of freelance peacemakers Yair Hirschfeld, a Middle East history professor at Haifa University, and Ahmed Kriah, head of the P.L.O.'s economics department (Hirschfeld violated Israeli law by speaking to Kriah). Their first meeting in a London hotel would lead to more than a dozen secret sessions in Norway that produced the biggest breakthrough in Middle East negotiations since Anwar Sadat made peace with Menachem Begin in 1978.

The declaration provided for Israel's withdrawal from the 140-sq.-mi. Gaza Strip, with its 770,000 Palestinians, and from Jericho, an ancient, somnolent Jordan Valley town of about 20,000, a thin sliver of the 1 million Palestinians who then lived in the West Bank.

Why peace now? Israel, like Rabin, was weary of the burden of being a garrison state and sick of administering the rebellious Palestinian lands. As for Arafat, his turnaround ironically was sired by weakness rather than strength. Young Palestinians were deserting

■ In the most dramatic movement toward peace since 1978's Camp David accords, bitter enemies clasp hands at the White House, and both Palestinian and Israeli hearts are lifted

HISTORY IS OFTEN THE RESIDUE of tanks and armies, of the victors and the vanquished. Sometimes it is the work of paper and pens. But when veteran antagonists Yasser Arafat and Yitzhak Rabin clasped hands in front of a beaming Bill Clinton on the White House lawn on Sept. 13, 1993, history was forged in a handshake. Caught in the click of hundreds of cameras, the seemingly unbelievable scene was beamed to millions of people in a world nurtured for 45 years on a diet of hate and death in the arid lands of the Middle East. This human touch, perhaps more than the Declaration of Principles

JOY! Left, Palestinian children celebrate the declaration of the Palestinian Authority. Below, Bill Clinton presides as ancient enemies resolve some of their differences at the White House

Arafat's Fatah party in favor of the more radical Hamas group, and with the decline of the U.S.S.R., he had lost his superpower patron, while his support of Iraq during the Gulf War cost him his bankrollers in the gulf states. At last, Arafat was prepared to settle for a little—and to a grateful world, that meant a lot. ■

MOURNING: Israelis gather to honor Rabin's memory

1995

Rabin Is Assassinated

■ In yet another victory for extremists, a Jewish militant murders Israel's great warrior for peace

SHIR HA-SHALOM (THE SONG OF PEACE). IN A rare moment of elation for the often dour leader of Israel, Yitzhak Rabin tucked a leaflet with the lyrics to the ancient song into his breast pocket and sang along with the 100,000 people who had gathered to support him on a November evening on Kings of Israel Square in the heart of Tel Aviv. "There are enemies of the peace process, and they try to hurt us," he told the crowd, as he urged them to proceed down the road to which he had committed Israel in September 1993. "But violence undermines democracy and must be denounced."

Moments later, after Rabin left the stage, a 25-year-old Jewish militant named Yigal Amir fired two shots into Rabin's back from only 8 ft. away. The hollow-point bullets smashed into Rabin, who had always refused to wear a bulletproof vest, drenching in blood the leaflet in his pocket, *Shir Ha-Shalom*.

News of the assassination sent thousands to the Western Wall in Jerusalem, the wall that Rabin had helped capture as the Israeli army's chief of staff in the Six-Day War of 1967. Born in Palestine in 1922, of Russian descent, Rabin had been a fighter all his life. As a young rebel against British rule, he was invited by the dynamic Moshe Dayan to join the Palmach, the élite strike force of the underground army Haganah during World War II.

Rabin fought with distinction in the War of Independence of 1948 and spent several years afterward in training, building and equipping the Israeli army, rising to become its chief of staff in 1964. In 1967 he prosecuted the Six- Day War brilliantly; later he served as Israel's ambassador to the U.S. and as Prime Minister from 1974 to 1977.

Rabin was Israel's Defense Minister during the Palestinian *intifadeh* of 1987, and he ultimately became convinced—grudgingly—that Israel would never rest while it tried to administer the hostile Palestinians. Elected Prime Minister again in 1992, he soon began the gutsy peace process that culminated in his famous handshake with Yasser Arafat at the White House in 1993.

In the two years that followed, the far reaches of Israel's radical right had grown bold in their threats to subvert the plan and preserve their dream of a Greater Israel, stretching to the Jordan River. For months, Rabin's Labor Party had complained that the opposition Likud Party, psychological compatriot of the extremists in its dislike of the peace plan, was fomenting an atmosphere in which someone might turn to violence. That someone was Amir. Once again, extremism had triumphed over moderation in the Middle East, in the language extremists best understand: the sound of gunfire. ■

1996

NOEL QUIDU—GAMMA PRESS

GOD'S GUERRILLAS: Taliban warriors show off their standard look: long beards, Kalashnikov rifles, scowls

Triumph of the Taliban

■ Radical students turned guerrillas seize power in Afghanistan and help foster a new era of Islamic terrorism

NOVEMBER 1996: THE SOUND OF ARTILLERY AND machine-gun fire reverberated in the darkened sky over Kabul, capital of war-weary Afghanistan. When dawn arrived, residents cautiously crept from their homes in search of clues as to who had won control of their city. Outside the presidential palace, they found the answer. Swinging from a concrete post were two discolored corpses: those of Najibullah, President of Afghanistan from 1987 to 1992, and his feared and hated brother, Shahpur Ahmedzi.

It was an appropriately medieval spectacle for a country that had years earlier degenerated into groups of primitive warlords' bands —although equipped with frighteningly modern weaponry. Najibullah's swinging body signified that Kabul had fallen to a new set of victors, the Taliban ("students," a reference to their study of the Koran). This two-year-old guerrilla group of former religious scholars had begun their march on the capital only two days earlier, culminating their two-year campaign to seize control of the country.

As the residents of Kabul gathered around, many cheered the gory spectacle—Najibullah had been nicknamed the "Butcher of Kabul" for his brutal, Soviet-backed rule, and his brother had served as his security chief. But the crowd was celebrating Najibullah's fall rather than the Taliban's rise. Apart from their severe Islamic fundamentalism, little was known about the Taliban or their mysterious leader, Mullah Mohammed Omar, a former *mujahedin,* or holy warrior, in his 30s who had fought the Soviets during the 1980s. One thing was certain: he had led the Taliban to a great victory, whose spoils were the chance to rule Afghanistan along lines laid down some 13 centuries before.

Hours after taking the city, the Taliban declared that "a complete Islamic system will be enforced." In their first week, the Taliban shut girls out of schools and ordered women workers to leave offices and hospitals. Men were given 45 days to grow a beard; cab drivers were told to pull up to a mosque five times a day to pray. Photographing the human figure was forbidden; music was banned; theft was punishable by cutting off a hand. Within a year, the Taliban were conducting so many public beatings, amputations and executions that they took over Kabul's old soccer stadium as a venue for their displays of Grand Guignol.

Even worse, the Taliban now flung open the doors of their nation to the Islamic world's most experienced jihadists, and Osama bin Laden, Ayman al-Zawahiri and the like were soon training bombers in the nation's hills. ■

1998

The U.S. Embassy Attacks

■ Al-Qaeda makes a stunning debut on the world stage with a well-timed, precision strike on two U.S. diplomatic outposts in Africa

ALTHOUGH SITUATED IN DIFFERENT COUNTRIES and separated by 450 miles, Nairobi, Kenya, and Dar es Salaam, Tanzania, are close enough to share the same weather. So the morning of Aug. 7, 1998, was similarly beautiful in both cities: sunny and cloudless, with a gentle breeze blowing in from the Indian Ocean. Both cities also experienced, at almost precisely the same moment, a nearly identical clap of thunder, flash of lightning and sudden dark cloud obscuring the morning light. But this storm was political, not meteorological: deadly bombs detonated at the U.S. embassies in both cities at 10:35 a.m.

The dual explosions bore a single message: the world's sole superpower still has enemies —secret, violent and determined. Despite your enormous wealth and strength, the bombers seemed to be saying, we can still inflict a great hurt. The mystery, of course, was why. Why there, and why then? In an earlier era of terrorism, the years of skyjackings and hostages and cross-border killings, the purpose was usually obvious, a bloody form of bargaining, and the killers trumpeted their responsibility; the message got across only if it was signed.

Yet more recent practitioners, like the men who leveled the U.S. military barracks in Saudi Arabia in 1996, rarely called in with their names or sought a discernible result. Theirs appeared to be acts of recruitment to win adherents to a fanatical cause, or of secret vengeance. Above all, the anonymous blasts from the blue seemed to be terrorism for terrorism's sake, intended to sow fear and make Americans tremble.

The new age of terrorism that the African embassy attacks inaugurated bore several hallmarks: sophisticated planning, large-scale loss of life (more than 250 people died at the two embassies) and tightly choreographed multiple attacks, carried out simultaneously with careful coordination. They were also the work of a man whose name few Americans had heard before: a wealthy, exiled Saudi living as a guest of the Taliban in a remote area of Afghanistan: Osama bin Laden. "All Muslims," he had said that May, "must declare jihad" against Americans.

In November, a U.S. court would indict bin Laden in absentia for conspiring in the plot to bomb the embassies, but President Bill Clinton sent him a message in return well before then. Two weeks after the embassy bombings, more than 60 Tomahawk cruise missiles rained down on bin Laden's terrorist training camps in Afghanistan; another 20 smashed into a building in Khartoum, Sudan, that U.S. intelligence officials believed was being used to make chemical weapons for bin Laden's group—although that claim would later be seriously disputed.

The first group of missiles found their mark, destroying several camps at which aspiring jihadists were rehearsing for future carnage. But the Tomahawks missed bin Laden himself by a few hours, ensuring that the U.S. and the world would hear from him again. ■

SHATTERED: Victims of the bomb blast at the U.S. embassy in Nairobi work to locate and save survivors. The deed left some 5,000 people injured and 213 dead

FRANCO PAGETTI—POLARIS

Intifadeh, Round Two

UPRISING: A Palestinian prepares to hurl a stone at Israeli lines in the West Bank city of Ramallah on Oct. 16, 2000

■ When Washington summit talks over the future of Jerusalem collapse, Yasser Arafat and Ariel Sharon spark a new round of rebellion

WHEN PRESIDENT BILL CLINTON INVITED Palestinian Authority President Yasser Arafat and Israeli Prime Minister Ehud Barak to join him at Camp David in July 2000 for a summit conference, hopes ran high for a sequel to the historic 1978 get-together when Israel and Egypt forged a peace plan at the presidential retreat in the Maryland mountains. But the summiteers failed to reach an agreement, and within a few months that failure was echoed in gunfire on the streets of the Middle East.

At the summit, Barak made an unprecedented offer concerning the disputed 35 acres in Jerusalem the Jews call Temple Mount and the Arabs know as Haram al-Sharif, or the Noble Sanctuary, site of the revered al-Aqsa Mosque. At Camp David, Barak proposed that Arafat assume control of the Islamic shrines but not take sovereignty over the site.

Arafat refused. Muslims must control their sacred site, he insisted—and the talks broke down. When Arafat returned to the Middle East, he ordered the leaders of his Fatah party's Tanzim militia to prepare for violence.

The fuse was ready to burn, and Ariel Sharon lit it: the leader of Israel's right-wing Likud Party visited the holy site on Sept. 28 in a demonstration of Israeli control over the land. Arabs saw Sharon's visit as an act of breathtaking arrogance and took to the streets in a new *intifadeh*. The violence crested on Oct. 12, when the gut-wrenching televised death of a Palestinian boy, shot as his father tried to shelter him from Israeli troops, ignited Arab passions; in response, two Israeli soldiers were killed and their bodies mutilated in Ramallah, and gun fighting and skirmishing rocked the Palestinian lands controlled by Israel.

Barak ordered a fast retaliation, sending Cobra attack helicopters to bomb five carefully chosen security sites, one of them close enough to rattle the Gaza headquarters of Arafat. The spiral of violence was under way. For the first time, Israeli Arabs, fed up with years of discrimination, joined in neighbor-to-neighbor mayhem within the confines of Israel itself. Tanzim forces launched a full-fledged shooting war on Israelis at night.

In the blink of an eye, the Middle East had moved backward. A region pregnant with hopes of peace—building since the 1993 Oslo Accords—was once again a place where proponents of peace were all but discredited. As body counts mounted on both sides, the greatest casualty was something just as fragile as a human life: the peace process itself. ■

Al-Qaeda Attacks the U.S.S. *Cole*

■ In another brazen act of terrorism, al-Qaeda operatives in Yemen bomb a U.S. Navy ship, killing 17 Americans

THE 300 MEN AND WOMEN ABOARD THE U.S.S. *Cole* had been at sea for two uneventful months when their vessel arrived in the harbor of Aden, Yemen, on Oct. 12, 2000. Unrest in the Middle East had trebled in recent weeks, amplified by the collapse of the Israeli-Palestinian summit talks at Camp David over the future of Jerusalem and the Sept. 28 visit by Israeli hard-liner Ariel Sharon to the disputed site of sacred Arab shrines in the Old City of East Jerusalem.

The *Cole* had arrived in the Middle East for a six-month mission with the Navy's Fifth Fleet in the Persian Gulf, where it would help enforce the international oil embargo against Iraq, in effect since 1991.

As the destroyer steamed into Aden Harbor just before noon, moving close to an offshore mooring station where it could refuel, crew members were on deck, armed and at attention. But they missed the threat. Several small boats approached to assist in attaching the *Cole's* thick 5-in. lines to fixed buoys. At 12:15, a small harbor boat mingling among the moorers pulled alongside. Two men stood upright, at attention, and their boat exploded.

The blast tore a 40-ft. by 40-ft. hole in the port side of the *Cole,* shoving one of the ship's decks upward and destroying an engine room and an adjoining mess area. Sailors not maimed by the explosion and flying shrapnel had only an instant to scramble to safety before water rushed into the gaping hole and engulfed them. As the *Cole,* a $1 billion destroyer armed with an assortment of high-caliber machine guns, missiles and advanced radar equipment, listed sickeningly to port, crew members worked furiously and managed to keep the ship afloat.

The attack killed 17 sailors and injured 38 more. The size of the blast, the perpetrators' ability to conceal the bomb and the advance knowledge of the *Cole's* plans suggested the attack was plotted well in advance. Within days, U.S. authorities believed it to be the work of the Middle East's most efficient purveyors of terror, Osama bin Laden's al-Qaeda network.

A measure of retaliation came two years after the attack: on Nov. 3, 2002, the CIA fired a Hellfire missile from a Predator drone aircraft, killing al-Qaeda operative Qaed Salim Sinan al-Hareth, suspected of leading the *Cole* attack, and five others as they rode in a vehicle some 100 miles east of Sana'a, Yemen's capital.

The attack on the *Cole,* following the al-Qaeda bombing of two U.S. embassies in Africa in 1998, should have been a wake-up call to Americans that bin Laden was now intent on staging larger and more spectacular attacks on the U.S. But domestic events soon drew Americans' attention elsewhere. Three weeks after the *Cole* was bombed, the U.S. presidential election ended in dispute, and the nation was transfixed by partisan politics and Supreme Court deliberations until Republican candidate George W. Bush was determined the winner in mid-December. Bush and his team took office Jan. 20, 2001; eight months later, al-Qaeda struck again—this time from the air, and this time against targets in the U.S. ■

2000

BOMBED: Heavily damaged in Yemen, the *Cole* was restored and returned to its home port in Newport News, Va., in April 2002

2001

America Under Assault

■ Middle East militants strike America, as al-Qaeda agents hijack four jets and launch a surprise attack on the U.S., plunging Americans into a new kind of battle: a war on terrorism

NO AMERICAN NEEDS TO READ A SUMMARY OF the events of Sept. 11, 2001—they are forever branded on the nation's psyche, a scar that has yet to heal. The enormity of those events—the hijacking of four jet airliners, two of which crashed into the World Trade Center in Manhattan, one of which hit the Pentagon and the last of which slammed into a Pennsylvania farm field after a

timely rebellion by its alerted passengers—made this day epochal, unforgettable, a Pearl Harbor for the 21st century.

And that, of course, was precisely the aim of the twisted but brilliant genius who was the begetter of those horrors, which claimed the lives of 2,973 innocent American civilians: Osama bin Laden. The al-Qaeda leader had already shown his flair for dramatic terrorism in a series of attacks on America abroad, including the bombing of two U.S. embassies in Africa in 1998 and of the U.S.S. *Cole* in 2000, only 11 months before the vicious four-pronged assault in 2001. After the embassy attacks, President Bill Clinton sent a flurry of Tomahawk missiles at one of bin Laden's terrorism training camps in Afghanistan; the al-Qaeda kingpin is thought to have escaped them by only an hour or so. A top-secret intelligence briefing placed in the hands of current President George W. Bush on Aug. 6, a month before

the attack, bore the heading "Bin Laden Determined to Strike in the U.S."

Despite those clues, which seemed so obvious in hindsight, the morning's attacks on the East Coast staggered Americans and their President. In Florida to push an education bill, Bush went aloft in Air Force One and spent much of the day flying to a succession of airbases, maintaining contact with the White House. The seemingly surreal stories of the day mounted, as Americans watched the Twin Towers of the World Trade Center collapse, cheered the heroism of ordinary Americans and public servants like New York City Mayor Rudolph Giuliani and pondered the bizarre crash of United Airlines Flight 93 in Pennsylvania, which was not understood until later to be the work of its valiant passengers.

That night the President returned to a capital that was buckled down as if in wartime, marched across the White House lawn and

ROBERT A. CUMINS—BLACK STAR

HORROR: With the north tower of New York City's World Trade Center already hit and smoking, the hijacked United Airlines Flight 175 is about to slam into the south tower on Sept. 11, 2001

addressed the nation on TV; the next day he branded the attacks "acts of war."

Americans were shocked and bewildered by the day's events. Not since the Civil War, 140 years before, had so much blood been spilled on their own soil. It was clear that the carefully coordinated attacks were the work of terrorists, but most Americans found it hard to fathom the intensity of the hatred that would lead the hijackers, 19 young men, to sacrifice their lives in order to wreak pain and suffering upon America. Across the land, neighbors asked each other: "why do they hate us?"

When it later emerged that 15 of the 19 hijackers were Saudis, like bin Laden, Americans were further confused. Although the U.S. and Saudi Arabia were divided by clear cultural and religious differences and had never seen eye to eye on the subject of Israel, the two had enjoyed a long alliance based on the mutual

interest of the oil trade, and the Arabs had often worked in tandem with the U.S. to promote moderation in the Middle East. Generations of U.S. executives and engineers had lived and worked in the Saudi oil fields, and thousands of Saudi students had come to the U.S. for higher education—not to turn jet airplanes into projectiles of horror.

President Bush rallied Americans again three days after the attack, when he visited the ruins of the Twin Towers in lower Manhattan— now a smoking heap of wreckage dubbed ground zero—grabbed a bullhorn and shouted to cheering rescue workers, "I can hear you. The rest of the world hears you. And the people who knocked these buildings down will hear all of us soon." On Sept. 20 Bush addressed a joint session of Congress and declared, "Whether we bring our enemies to justice or bring justice to our enemies, justice will be done." The vast majority of his listen-

ers, wounded and grieving, were prepared to rally behind him. And a shocked world also rushed to the U.S. side, denouncing the terrorists and their deeds and vowing to stand by the U.S. in its pursuit of its foes.

By now, there was no doubt as to who those enemies were: bin Laden and his No. 2 man, Ayman al-Zawahiri, the Egyptian physician who had left a trail of terror across the Middle East for decades. The two had coordinated the attack, using bin Laden's wealth and relying on the carefully coordinated terrorism organization he had built in recent years, from the safe harbors provided them by the radical Taliban faction that had run Afghanistan since 1996.

Now all eyes turned to Afghanistan and the Middle East, as the Bush Administration and the Pentagon prepared to fight a new kind of war that would lead the U.S. into its closest engagement with the Middle East in history: a war on terrorism.

The U.S. Topples the Taliban

■ Shocked by the deadly 9/11 terrorist attacks, an allied coalition puts the Taliban to flight, but al-Qaeda kingpin Osama bin Laden slips away

MORE THAN TWO WEEKS AGO," PRESIDENT George W. Bush told Americans on Oct. 7, 2001, "I gave Taliban leaders a series of clear and specific demands: close terrorist training camps; hand over leaders of the al-Qaeda network; and return all foreign nationals, including American citizens, unjustly detained in your country. None of these demands were met. And now the Taliban will pay a price."

Before the first bomb was dropped, however—indeed little more than a week after Osama bin Laden's Afghan-based al-Qaeda network rocked the world with the 9/11 terrorist attacks on America—U.S. special forces troops, wearing turbans and beards rather than regulation uniforms, had begun slipping into Afghanistan. Accompanied by CIA guides, armed with high-tech targeting equipment to guide bombs and missiles and carrying suitcases full of cash with which to entice tribal chieftains away from the Taliban, they fanned out through the countryside.

The U.S. agents directed a flood of money and weapons to the Northern Alliance, a coalition of anti-Taliban warlords and regional chiefs that began to aggressively engage Taliban forces. Seeing what was coming, Taliban leader Mullah Omar had already gone into hiding; days later, forces loyal to him began withdrawing from villages around the coun-

try, often under attack from vengeful locals who had endured Taliban cruelty for years.

Operation Enduring Freedom officially began a few hours before Bush's speech, as bombs and missiles hit targets around the country. The Taliban grip on power unraveled quickly. The capital of Kabul fell on Nov. 12, followed in short order by other major cities: Jalalabad, Herat, Konduz. By late November the Taliban were completely surrounded in their stronghold of Kandahar. But they escaped,

led by Mullah Omar, into the mountains and caves of the Tora Bora region near the Pakistan border. Here the U.S. troops appeared to have trapped their foremost prey, bin Laden, but the elusive jihadist slipped from their clutches, escaping by perhaps only a few hours.

By the first days of 2002, the war was finished, and control of Afghanistan passed to the coalition of allies assembled by Bush—although, as the Soviets learned in the 1980s, real control of the Afghans' tribal society gen-

FREE! Afghan children cheer as Northern Alliance tanks roll into the capital city of Kabul

erally rests with its regional warlords.

In the years since the Taliban were toppled, as the U.S. focused on its intervention in Iraq, Taliban fighters have emerged from the mountains and caves to stage ambushes, commit acts of terrorism and challenge the nation's new leader, Hamid Karzai. As of the fall of 2006, more than 300 Americans have died fighting in Afghanistan—and neither Mullah Omar nor his terrorist guest, bin Laden, has been captured.　■

PAULA BRONSTEIN—GETTY IMAGES

Karzai in 2001

Hamid Karzai

The future President of Afghanistan cut a curious figure in the waning days of Taliban rule. In November 2001, when he rode a motorcycle from Quetta, Pakistan, into southern Afghanistan to help launch the uprising against the Taliban, he was unarmed and had only his credential as a tribal chief to protect him. At the time, friends told Karzai his plan was suicidal, that he might as well save the gas money and drive his bike straight into a brick wall.

In the months that followed, al-

though he was one of the few people in the country without a gun, Karzai tamed perhaps the world's most lawless land—not through force but with charm, diplomacy and guts.

When he started showing up unarmed in the mountain villages of Oruzgan province to preach against the Taliban in their very stronghold, tribal elders listened, even though they were probably dazzled less by his convictions than his courage. Afghans admire the valorous—and the victorious. When Karzai turned out to be both, he became every warlord's second choice to lead the country, after himself.

Born in Kandahar and educated in India, the pro-Western Pashtun nobleman glides easily between the traditional and the modern worlds. In the manner of Afghan chieftains, he allows everyone to have his say, then firmly imposes his will. "We talk, I get mad at them, they get mad at me, we joke a little, and then, finally, we agree," he says of his approach to leading a fractious pack of power brokers motivated primarily by personal greed and tribal ambitions. "That's the Afghan way."

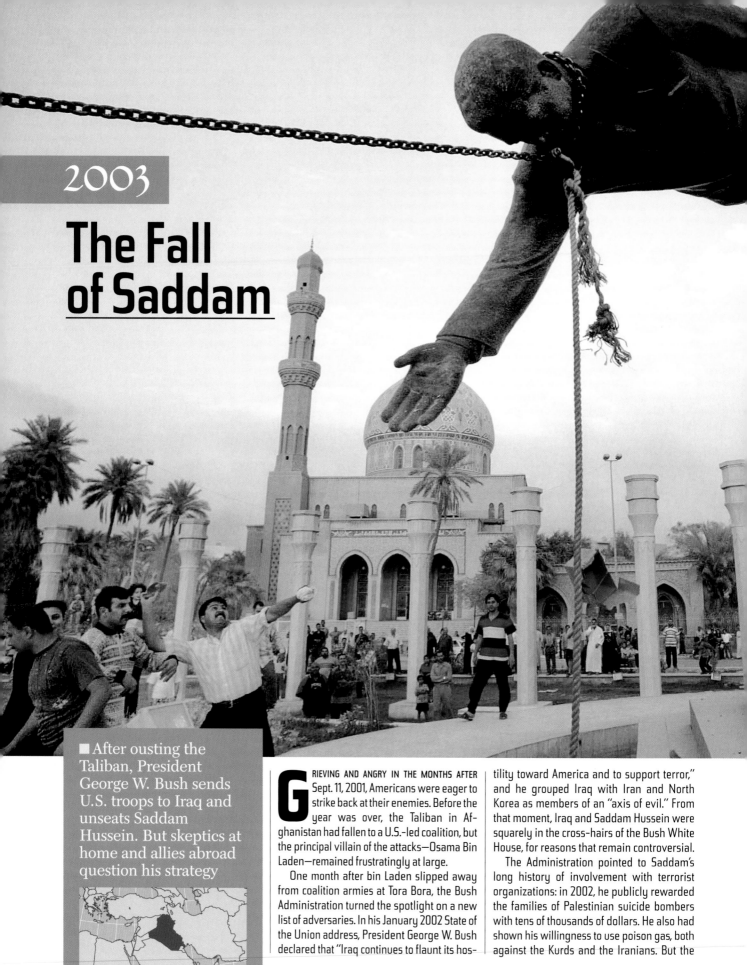

2003

The Fall of Saddam

■ After ousting the Taliban, President George W. Bush sends U.S. troops to Iraq and unseats Saddam Hussein. But skeptics at home and allies abroad question his strategy

GRIEVING AND ANGRY IN THE MONTHS AFTER Sept. 11, 2001, Americans were eager to strike back at their enemies. Before the year was over, the Taliban in Afghanistan had fallen to a U.S.-led coalition, but the principal villain of the attacks—Osama Bin Laden—remained frustratingly at large.

One month after bin Laden slipped away from coalition armies at Tora Bora, the Bush Administration turned the spotlight on a new list of adversaries. In his January 2002 State of the Union address, President George W. Bush declared that "Iraq continues to flaunt its hos-

tility toward America and to support terror," and he grouped Iraq with Iran and North Korea as members of an "axis of evil." From that moment, Iraq and Saddam Hussein were squarely in the cross-hairs of the Bush White House, for reasons that remain controversial.

The Administration pointed to Saddam's long history of involvement with terrorist organizations: in 2002, he publicly rewarded the families of Palestinian suicide bombers with tens of thousands of dollars. He also had shown his willingness to use poison gas, both against the Kurds and the Iranians. But the

DECLINING: Iraqis cheer the toppling of a statue of Saddam in Baghdad on April 13, 2003; his regime fell almost as easily to the small U.S.-led coalition

most important and most oft-repeated charge was that Saddam was building weapons of mass destruction. His government had a long, well-documented history of trying to acquire both nuclear and biological weapons. But actual evidence that Saddam was still acting on this desire, more than a decade later, was hard to come by.

Bush's reasons for demanding Saddam's removal in Iraq, however compelling at first glance, were disturbingly short on specific, verifiable detail. Skeptics asked which changed

circumstances or new information made Iraq suddenly more dangerous or war with Saddam suddenly more necessary. No one on Bush's team was prepared to explain what exactly Iraq had to do with bin Laden, and Bush's critics wondered whether that wasn't the point: tracking down al-Qaeda's chief might take years, but Iraq seemed a comparatively easy target at which to vent U.S. anger.

Either way, a drum roll of events signaled the new policy. Bush devoted much of the year 2002 to painting Saddam's Iraq as an outlaw nation that was developing weapons of mass destruction. Bush urged America's allies and the U.N. to demand a robust new round of inspections to assess Iraq's arsenal—and made it clear that if Saddam did not agree, the U.S. was prepared to go to war to disarm him. Moreover, Bush declared, he was prepared to wage that war alone, if necessary.

By year's end, Bush got his way: U.N. inspectors were in Iraq, probing for weapons caches, and both houses of Congress had passed a resolution authorizing the President to use military force in Iraq, with or without U.N. approval. A buildup of U.S. forces brought more than 30,000 Americans in uniform to within striking distance of Iraq by the first week in December, with another 45,000 ready to join them on short notice.

In the first months of 2003, Bush formally ordered the U.S. military to begin planning for war in Iraq, even as U.N. inspectors reported, in essence, that while they couldn't find any proof that Iraq was still building weapons of mass destruction, neither could they find any proof that it wasn't. Yet in his January 2003 State of the Union address, the President cited reports that Iraq had tried to buy weapons-grade uranium from Niger. (Those reports turned out to be unfounded, and critics later charged that U.S. intelligence agencies had known they were false even as the President used them as a justification for the war.)

During this period, U.S. Secretary of State Colin Powell sought to build support for regime change in Iraq, making two major presentations to the U.N. in which he laid out the U.S. charges against Saddam. Britain, under Prime Minister Tony Blair, came onboard early. But longtime U.S. allies France and Germany found the arguments unpersuasive, as did U.N. heavyweights Russia and China.

Finally, on March 5, Powell said that the U.S. would, lead "a coalition of willing nations" to disarm Iraq, with or without U.N. approval. The following day, Bush declared at a news conference that U.N. authorization was unneces-

sary, saying, "We really don't need anybody's permission" to defend U.S. interests. The U.S. coalition declared that March 17 was the deadline for Iraq to prove that it had fully disarmed or face war.

When Saddam didn't move, coalition forces did, launching an unsuccessful "decapitation" strike on a Baghdad bunker thought to be harboring Saddam, unleashing a "shock and awe" aerial campaign against Baghdad and sending troops into Iraq. Within 24 hours, U.S. forces had captured the major oil fields in southern Iraq and had begun advancing on Baghdad. In the first week of the campaign, the fiercest resistance came not from Iraqi troops but from a howling desert sandstorm that halted the U.S. advance in its tracks.

By April 4, American troops had captured Saddam International Airport, 10 miles from Baghdad; three days later, U.S. tanks were roaming at will through Baghdad and British troops finally took the southern stronghold of Basra. On April 9, ecstatic crowds toppled a 40-ft.-tall statue of Saddam (with an assist from U.S. soldiers) and two days later, U.S. General Tommy Franks of Central Command declared, "The Saddam regime has ended."

The widespread looting and violent confrontations between angry Iraqi crowds and U.S. troops that followed didn't detract from the easy victory: the number of coalition dead was 169; the number of Iraqi dead was estimated at 3,000. U.S. Secretary of Defense Donald Rumsfeld told U.S. troops during an April 29 visit to Baghdad, "You've liberated a people, you've deposed a cruel dictator, and you have ended his threat to free nations."

But what were meant to be the last words on victory in Iraq were uttered by Rumsfeld's boss, George W. Bush. The former National Guard pilot flew an S-38 fighter aboard the aircraft carrier U.S.S. *Abraham Lincoln* on May 1, and declared in a nationally televised speech, "Major combat operations in Iraq have ended ... the United States and our allies have prevailed." The sense of victory was buttressed when U.S. forces killed Saddam's two sons, Uday and Qusay, in a July shootout, and with the capture of Saddam himself in December.

Aboard the *Lincoln,* the President declared, "Our coalition is engaged in securing and reconstructing that country [Iraq]." What it would take to accomplish this goal, how long the mission would last, and whether it was even possible—those questions didn't seem pressing at that euphoric moment. Before long, they would be impossible to ignore. ■

2003~06

The Insurgency: Meltdown in Iraq

■ Now for the hard part: after a swift victory over Saddam Hussein, coalition troops attempt to bring stability and a democratic government to Iraq—but are opposed by a multitude of foes waging a guerrilla war

ONE WEEK AFTER PRESIDENT GEORGE W. BUSH declared that major combat operations in Iraq had come to an end, Army Private First Class Marlin Rockhold, of Hamilton, Ohio, was directing traffic on a Baghdad bridge when he was shot and killed by a sniper. The same day, an Iraqi calmly walked up to another U.S. soldier on a second bridge and shot him to death. Five days later, Air Force Sergeant Patrick Lee Griffin was killed when the convoy he was travelling in was ambushed by Iraqi insurgents.

In the heady days after the coalition victory, it was easy to dismiss such incidents as the death rattle of a bloody conflict. But within weeks, a pattern of suicide bombings, sniper attacks and roadside ambushes began to emerge in occupied Iraq. The war may have been won, but it apparently wasn't over.

Indeed, rather than trailing off, the attacks grew in frequency and ferocity in the months that followed. Even more disturbing to military commanders, the strikes also grew in sophistication. What had begun as a series of random, sporadic incidents increasingly became coordinated and carefully planned raids. By late June 2003, Deputy Defense Secretary Paul Wolfowitz was describing the ongoing conflict in Iraq as "a guerrilla war."

The problem stemmed in part from unrealistic expectations. Both U.S. planners and Iraqi citizens seem to have imagined that once the war had been won, the country would quickly

CHAOS: Civilians in Baghdad react to a car bombing that killed 35 people and wounded hundreds more on Sept. 30, 2004

massacred 24 innocent Iraqis near the town of Haditha. Such atrocities outraged Iraqis who might otherwise have been inclined to view the U.S. cause with sympathy. And the failure to find evidence that Saddam had been harboring weapons of mass destruction undermined the Bush team's rationale for the war.

To be sure, there were successes. The June 2004 handover of sovereignty to Iraqis, elections in January and December 2005 and the drafting and ratification of a new Iraqi constitution in the fall of 2005 marked real progress toward a stable Iraqi government. The capture of Saddam in December 2003 and his appearance in a Baghdad courtroom in the summer of 2005 encouraged the belief that justice was being served in Iraq. And the handful of battles that took place whenever U.S. forces could find and pin down large concentrations of insurgents invariably resulted in lopsided victories.

By September 2004, when the U.S. death toll passed 1,000, the mayhem was taking on a new character: it was now divided primarily between Shi'ite and Sunni militias—the latter increasingly led by al-Qaeda kingpin Abu Mousab al-Zarqawi—intent more on killing their sectarian foes than U.S. troops. (The full death toll of Iraqi civilians is unknown, but it is estimated to run into many tens of thousands.) The internecine fighting was ratcheted up several notches in February 2006, when the Shi'ites' most revered shrine in Iraq, the golden-domed Askariya Mosque in Samarra, was bombed. More than 1,000 Iraqis died in Sunni-Shi'ite combat in the next week.

Americans savored a much needed win in June 2006, when al-Zarqawi was killed in a U.S. air attack that specifically targeted him. But this did not offset the grim reality on the ground. At the end of August, 2006, General George Casey, the commanding U.S. general in Iraq, estimated that Iraqi security forces would need another 12 to 18 months before they could take over from U.S. troops.

As of late 2006, the Bush Administration faced hard questions in Iraq. Could political success be salvaged from a military fight that might be unwinnable? Could the U.S. extract itself without harming its interests in the region? Could Shi'ites, Kurds and Sunnis, trained in the school of enmity, ever embrace a common destiny? As the roll call of American deaths in Iraq neared 3,000, and polls showed 63% of Americans were displeased with the White House's handling of the war, the answers were unclear. But it was clear that those deaths carried a price tag—more time and more sacrifice—that the U.S. public seemed increasingly hesitant to pay. ∎

blossom into a free-market democracy. Instead, occupation authorities struggled to police Iraq's streets, restore water and electricity, rebuild schools, monitor local elections and nudge Iraq toward democracy—all while waging a 24/7 campaign against increasingly brazen groups of militants.

When the high hopes fostered by Saddam Hussein's downfall didn't pan out, the enthusiasm of many Iraqis expired. "At least we had power and security [under Saddam]," said a shop owner in Baghdad. "Democracy is not feeding us."

Who was behind the attacks? They were the work of the full spectrum of Iraqis with some reason to be angry or unhappy: humiliated (and heavily armed) former soldiers from the Iraqi army, disbanded by a U.S. directive; Shi'ites long oppressed by Saddam and now thirsting for both power and revenge; Sunnis furious at being displaced from their long monopoly on power—and that list includes only domestic opponents. Factor in the legions of "foreign fighters" slipping into the country from Iran, Syria, Saudi Arabia and elsewhere in the Arab world to wage jihad against the U.S., and the odds began to look long indeed.

By early 2004, as the U.S. death toll passed 500, the insurgents were profiting from a series of tragic U.S. missteps. In April, photographs of prisoner abuse by U.S. soldiers at Abu Ghraib prison became public. Nineteen months later, in November 2005, U.S. Marines allegedly

CRY FOR HELP: Moments after the bombing that killed Hariri and 21 others, a bystander calls for aid

MAHAMED AZAKIR—REUTERS—LANDOV

Murder in Lebanon

■ A moderate leader is killed in Beirut, and pro-Western Lebanese briefly glimpse a future free from Syrian control

RAFIK HARIRI WAS A SELF-MADE BILLIONAIRE, a Lebanese Sunni Muslim who made a huge fortune in construction, oil, real estate, banking and telecommunications, then turned his attention to politics. After helping broker the 1989 Taif accord that ended the bloody civil war that lasted from 1975 to 1990, Hariri served a term as Prime Minister from 1992 to 1998, then came to power again in 2000, resigning in October 2004.

In his years in office, Hariri, an ally of the Saudi royal family and the government of France, played a key role in reconstructing his battered nation, which was reduced to rubble during the civil war. Gleaming hotels and apartment towers sprang up on Beirut's famed Corniche along the Mediterranean; the city was once again the Paris of the Middle East.

But Hariri was forced to accept a devil's bargain to retain his grip on power: he allowed Syria's longtime strongman Hafez Assad to keep troops within Lebanon and boss its politics through his proxy group, the militant Hizballah party. No friend to Israel, Hariri refused to hand over Hizballah agents identified as terrorists by the U.S. and Israel. Even so, by the harsh standards of the Middle East, he was a moderate rather than an extremist.

Above all, Hariri was a champion of Lebanon. After Assad's death in 2000, Hariri began to pursue his dream of freeing his nation from its neighbor's grasp. That policy probably sealed his death warrant: on Feb. 14, 2005, a thunderous blast struck his armor-plated convoy of cars as it passed the St. George Hotel on the Corniche, killing Hariri and 16 others.

Hariri's murder galvanized Lebanon's pro-Western citizens, leading to an unprecedented show of opposition to Syria, in three memorable days of massive street protests. Hizballah chieftain Hassan Nasrallah soon retaliated with even larger pro-Syria demonstrations. But proponents of Lebanon's "Cedar Revolution" seem to have won a major victory when Assad's son and heir Bashar withdrew all Syrian troops from Lebanon on April, 26, 2005. Pro-Syrian P.M. Omar Karami soon resigned—although his Syria-friendly government was quickly back in power.

A United Nations inquiry led by Irish police commissioner Peter FitzGerald laid blame for the murder on Syria's hegemony over Lebanon. The U.N. team could not name his killers, however, claiming that Lebanese security forces controlled by Syria thwarted its work.

By the summer of 2006, Hariri's murder was no longer viewed as having ushered in a brave new age of Lebanese independence. As Israeli troops and Hizballah militiamen fought to control Lebanon's future, and Hariri's rebuilt Beirut lay in shambles, the Cedar Revolution of 2005 seemed to lie in ruins as well, another victim of the fanatically divisive hatreds of the modern Middle East. ■

New Day For Gaza

■ Voluntarily giving up its settlements in Gaza, Israel trades land for security—but later events dampen the effects of the withdrawal

THE DEATH OF YASSER ARAFAT IN NOVEMBER 2004 offered the rare chance for a fresh start in the Middle East, and two men quickly acted to seize the day. One was Arafat's hand-picked successor, Mahmoud Abbas, the new President of the Palestinian Authority (P.A.); the other was Israel's Prime Minister, Ariel Sharon, the once uncompromising hawk who, like his fellow soldiers Moshe Dayan and Yitzhak Rabin before him, had become a proponent of compromise.

Both leaders gambled their fate on Israel's 2004 pledge to begin withdrawing, in July 2005, from the Gaza Strip territories it had held since the Six-Day War in 1967. Each fought off dissenters in his own ranks. Sharon's coalition in the Knesset disintegrated in early January, and he had to patch together a new one. Abbas struggled to tame armed factions, such as Hamas and Islamic Jihad, that owed him no allegiance and were opposed to any truce with Israel.

Yet Sharon and Abbas forged ahead, meeting at a summit meeting in Egypt's Sharm el-Sheikh resort on Feb. 8, 2005, where Israel reaffirmed its commitment to the Gaza pullout, promised to release several hundred Palestinian prisoners and also agreed to resume a limited handover of towns in the West Bank.

Weeks later, Abbas convened a Palestinian summit at which Hamas and Islamic Jihad agreed to work within the framework of the Abbas plan and promised to replace the *intifadeh* with a *tahediyeh* (truce). Israel later agreed to suspend its program of targeted assassinations of Hamas leaders. As optimism swelled, President George W. Bush welcomed Abbas to the White House in May, where he pledged $50 million in direct aid to the Palestinians, a first for the U.S.

On Aug. 15, Israel's army began a forced evacuation of remaining Jewish settlers within Gaza and resumed the transfer of control in four West Bank villages. By Sept. 1, all 21 Jewish settlements had been completely emptied without major incident, the last Israeli soldiers had left Gaza, and 38 years of occupation had come to an end.

If the moment was inspiring, the days that followed were disappointing. Hamas leaders paraded large formations of heavily armed fighters through the settlements, declaring that their armed struggle (rather than Abbas' negotiations) had wrested Gaza from Israel, trashed synagogues and greenhouses and pronounced themselves in charge of the area. Militant groups resumed firing rockets into Israel, and chaos broke out on the Egyptian border. None of this augured well for the P.A.'s ability to someday govern a sovereign state.

Even so, Israel's willingness to withdraw from Gaza was a strong sign that the 2003 "road map" envisioned by Sharon and the Bush Administration to settle the long conflict between Israel and the Palestinians was viable. Yet within a year, this harbinger of promise would seem illusory. Sharon was felled by a stroke in January 2006; later that month, Hamas, not Abbas' Fatah party, was victorious in Palestinian elections. By summer, Israeli troops were battling Hizballah militia in Lebanon. Once again in the Middle East, the forces of division proved to be stronger than the forces of peace. ■

RESIST! On Aug. 18, Israeli settlers barricaded on the roof of a synagogue in Gaza battle government troops training water cannons on them

2005

MAN OF THE HOUR: Ahmadinejad with members of the Basij militia at a rally in Tehran on May 7, 2006

Iran's New Leader

■ A committed Islamic fundamentalist wins a stunning victory in Iran's national election, and the country takes a turn to the right, as it seeks nuclear power— and Israel's extinction

HARD-LINER IS NOT A NICE WORD, EVEN FOR hard-liners. So, immediately after his surprising landslide victory in Iran's June 25, 2005, national election, Mahmoud Ahmadinejad declared that as his nation's new President, he would not be shutting Iran off from the rest of the world or curtailing the Internet or taking the country back to the 9th century. His Iran, said the erstwhile mayor of Tehran, would be modern and strong (meaning nuclear powered) and rich, with prosperity to be shared among all classes, not just the élite.

Fine words. Yet that night, the streets of Tehran's better-off northern districts were like a ghost town full of zombies, with residents in shock over the accession of a little-known revolutionary and Islamic zealot. "We are doomed," said Nasser Soroudi, 33, a salesman at a photo shop. He, like many of his countrymen, feared that the new President would turn their country into "Taliban-land."

Ahmadinejad defeated the wily political veteran Ayatullah Ali Akbar Hashemi Rafsanjani, 70, who ran on a pragmatic platform that promised a tilt to the West. But Rafsanjani could not consolidate support from the country's progressive voters, who were wary of his family's largely unexplained wealth and unhappy about the corruption that grew under his watch as President from 1989 to 1997. So while Iran's poorer classes, Islamic militias and web of religious social-action groups provided Ahmadinejad with 62% of the votes, Rafsanjani could muster only 36%, even in a country where many younger people—more than 50% of the population—claimed they preferred liberalization to fundamentalism.

The biggest winner in the election may have been Iran's Supreme Leader, Ayatullah Ali Khamenei. Since succeeding to the head of the theocracy with the death of Ayatullah Ruhollah Khomeini in 1989, Khamenei had always had to contend with rival conservatives like Rafsanjani or with reformist Mohammed Khatami, who had held the office since the end of Rafsanjani's term. While the presidency had always been a less powerful office than that of the Supreme Leader, it had been a strategic bully pulpit for those with ideas different from the theocracy. No more.

Since taking office, Ahmadinejad has done his best to irritate the West. He has defied threats of sanctions to stop developing his nuclear program, which he insists is intended for peaceful use. He made headlines around the world when he said of Israel, "[It] must be wiped off the map ..." And after the Israeli-Hizballah conflict in Lebanon in the summer of 2006, he sent millions of dollars in aid to his Hizballah allies in Lebanon.

Ahmadinejad has also shown a gift for the grand propaganda gesture. In May 2006, he wrote a rambling 18-page letter to George W. Bush, in which he praised Jesus Christ and condemned U.S. support for Israel; he received no reply. Months later he invited Bush to engage in a live TV debate; Bush declined. As for Iran's increasingly belligerent President, there is little debate: he is a confirmed, hard-line enemy of the U.S. and the West. ■

Hamas Wins at the Polls

■ The U.S. works to bring democracy to the Palestinians—but is shocked when voters overwhelmingly prefer the terrorist-allied Hamas Party to the moderate Fatah Party

BE CAREFUL WHAT YOU WISH FOR: ONE OF THE stated goals of Bush Administration policy in the Middle East is to foster democracy in the region. Yet in a series of stunning setbacks, elections held in 2005 and '06 in Iran, Iraq and the Palestinian territories brought politicians and parties hostile to U.S. intentions into power.

One of the biggest shocks was the victory of the militant Hamas Party in the Palestinian Legislative Council elections, held on Jan. 25, 2006. The militant group, long associated with terrorist attacks on Israel, won a landslide victory, taking 76 seats in the 132-seat parliament; the moderate ruling Fatah Party, founded by Yasser Arafat and now run by Mahmoud Abbas, won 43 seats; 13 went to fringe parties.

Hamas leaders immediately declared their first task would not involve confronting Israel but instead would be "cleaning the Palestinian house": the Palestinian Authority had been riddled with rampant corruption, the streets of the West Bank squalid and chaotic.

A reeling White House seized on that theme to explain the vote, arguing that it represented a rejection of Fatah's corruption rather than the peace process itself. Speaking at a press conference the morning after the vote, President Bush called the Hamas win a "wake-up call" for Fatah, saying, "You see, when you give people the vote ... and they're unhappy with the status quo, they'll let you know."

The Palestinians definitely sent a message: topping the Hamas electoral slate was Marwan Barghouti, a leader who had long insisted on the right to wage "armed struggle" to end the Israeli occupation and was residing in a jail cell in Israel on a terrorism charge.

Yet some found a note of hope in the Hamas victory, including TIME analyst Tony Karon, who observed, "When the two sides inevitably meet over a bargaining table—and history's lesson is that when national conflicts are solved in negotiations, those deemed terrorists eventually end up at that table—Israel will find Hamas a far tougher but also far more credible interlocutor than Arafat ever was. Just as the hard-liner Sharon was widely held to be the best Israeli leader to uproot settlements—not unlike Nixon going to China—so may Hamas well turn out to be the best bet for enforcing a truce." Encouraging words—but be careful what you wish for. ■

VICTORY! Hamas supporters celebrate their triumph at the polls on election night in Gaza City

Israel and Hizballah Go to War

■ A hostage drama escalates into the first full-tilt war in the Middle East in years, as Israel invades Lebanon and Hizballah fights back. Can a U.N. peace plan stop the hostilities?

PAVEL WOLBERG—EPA

EARLY SUMMER, 2006: THE SITUATION WAS NORmal in the Gaza Strip: all fouled up. Palestinian militants in the 28-mile-long sliver of land along the Mediterranean—which, with 1.4 million inhabitants is the planet's most densely populated area—had been firing homemade rockets at nearby Israeli towns for months and drawing artillery barrages in response. For the region, that was everyday life. But tensions escalated early in June after seven members of a Palestinian family died in a Gaza beach explosion, which

Palestinians blamed on an errant Israeli artillery shell. On June 25, in response, Hamas militants tunneled under the border between Gaza and Israel and kidnapped Israeli corporal Gilad Shalit, 19. A spiral of violence had been triggered: Israel bombed bridges and roads inside Gaza and destroyed six transformers at the central power plant, cutting off electricity to 45% of the territory's inhabitants.

Soon the Lebanese militant group Hizballah entered the fray: on July 12 members of the group crossed the border into Israel, killed eight Israeli soldiers and took two hostages. Ehud Olmert, who had served as Israel's Prime Minister for only six months following a January stroke that felled Ariel Sharon, acted vigorously. Calling the taking of the hostages "an act of war," he ordered air attacks on Hizballah positions in Lebanon—1,000 of them within 24 hours—as well as limited ground incursions.

Olmert's robust response appeared to be aimed not only at punishing Hizballah but also

at reshaping Israel's neighborhood. For the past six years, Israel had followed a policy of disengaging from hostile areas, trading land for peace. In 2000 it withdrew from the security zone it had occupied in southern Lebanon for 18 years; in 2005 it uprooted its settlers in Gaza. Yet in the six years since Israel's withdrawal from Lebanon, Israelis had watched Hizballah build fortifications along the border and stockpile rockets and missiles, while the group's charismatic leader, Hassan Nasrallah, explicitly threatened to kidnap Israeli soldiers.

Olmert's Cabinet backed his aggressive response, agreeing it was time to hit back, hard, to demonstrate that Israel was willing to fight. The message was aimed at Hizballah and also at Hamas and at Iran, which sponsors Hizballah and supports Hamas.

Yet to Israel's surprise, Hizballah didn't look for a way out: it launched an escalation of its own, shooting longer-range missiles than it

AT WAR: Israeli troops prepare to fire on Hizballah positions in Lebanon on July 13. By the war's end, an estimated 1,500 people were dead on both sides and some 1 million Lebanese and 500,000 Israelis had been driven from their homes

Israel's Prime Minister in 2006

Ehud Olmert

Elected Israel's Prime Minister in March 2006 in the wake of his predecessor Ariel Sharon's debilitating stroke, Ehud Olmert, 60, did not expect to define himself through military action. Voters brought him to power as a man explicitly committed to disengaging from Israel's foes, to walling them off by establishing borders marked by an imposing fence.

The former mayor of Jerusalem had once opposed the Camp David accords; as a young politician, he was so conscious of his sparse military background when contrasted with previous Israeli leaders that he enrolled for more army training at age 35, even as he was a member of the Knesset.

Hizballah's leader in 2006

Hassan Nasrallah

By the standards of Arab strongmen, Sheik Hassan Nasrallah, 46, is a charmer. In TV appearances during the '06 crisis in Lebanon, he appeared more soothing than bellicose, even flashing a smile now and then. But he's tough: after becoming Hizballah's chief at age 32 in 1992, he led a merciless guerrilla campaign that ended in Israel's withdrawal from Lebanon in 2000; his eldest son was killed by Israeli shelling in 1997.

In recent years, Nasrallah has cemented Hizballah's ties to its powerful sponsors, Iran and Syria. The group receives as much as $300 million a year from Tehran, and Nasrallah is a confidant of Syrian President Bashar Assad's.

ever had before into Israel, forcing the 1 million Israelis in the north of the country—a sixth of the nation's population—into bomb shelters.

In the weeks that followed, Israeli aircraft and artillery pummeled Beirut. At one point, Israeli forces dropped 23 tons of bombs on a bunker in Beirut where they believed Nasrallah was hiding; he survived. Meanwhile, on July 22, Israel sent 2,000 troops and tanks across the border to invade Lebanon; by the conflict's end, some 10,000 Israeli troops were in Lebanon. Yet Israel was doing more damage to Lebanese civilians and infrastructure—and to its own reputation—than to Hizballah.

Israel's strategy was complicated by the fact that Hizballah is more than simply a band of guerrillas: the group functions as a political party and has a representative in the Lebanese Cabinet. The Lebanese government and army are too weak to take on the group and its patrons, including Syria, a country that long dominated and still influences Lebanon.

As hundreds of thousands of Lebanese fled their homes and northern Israelis hunkered down in bomb shelters, Israel took a beating in the court of world opinion. Critics charged its response was far out of proportion to the initial provocation. Meanwhile, Hizballah portrayed its survival as a major victory, and that opinion was shared by an unexpected source, the Israeli public. A strong majority of Israelis had supported Olmert's aggressive strategy early on, but as the war escalated, more and more Israelis began to regard it as a mistake, and Olmert's grip on power was threatened.

On Aug. 15, following intense international diplomacy and several visits to the region by U.S. Secretary of State Condoleezza Rice, Israeli troops began withdrawing from Lebanon; most had left that nation by Aug. 25. The pullout was part of a deal approved by the U.N. Security Council on Aug. 11. Under Resolution 1701, a cease-fire went into effect, Hizballah

agreed to disarm, Israel agreed to withdraw its troops, and a force made up of Lebanese troops and U.N. peacekeepers would patrol a buffer zone between Lebanon and Israel. France, Spain, the U.S. and Turkey were among nations committing troops to the force.

Amid Lebanon's ruins, a war for hearts and minds emerged. Having claimed victory, Hizballah mobilized to win the peace: Nasrallah went on TV to promise that the Party of God would give $10,000 to all Lebanese whose homes had been damaged; the funds came straight from Tehran. Hizballah engineers in baseball caps reading JIHAD OF CONSTRUCTION went to work. On the other side of the fence, the Saudis, worried about the rise of militant groups in Iran and Iraq, provided $1 billion in funds to Lebanon's central banks and $500 million more in humanitarian aid. If Israelis and Hizballah must contend, a race to rebuild Lebanon is a welcome place to begin. ∎

Eight Questions for
The Middle East

ISOLATED: The Israeli settlement of Har Homa in East Jerusalem is a shining city on a hill—enclosed in barbed wire and protected by a security barrier

Q. SAKAMAKI/REDUX

Can Israel Be Accepted?

The nation of Israel—subject of the dreams of a people long scattered in Diaspora—became a reality in 1948. Yet this country has seen many nightmares in its brief lifetime. Today only four other nations in the region—Egypt, Jordan, Turkey and Qatar—even recognize its existence. Can Arab nations ever welcome the "Zionist entity" as an equal?

Can the Cycle of
Terrorism Be Stopped?

When Palestinian boys seek role models, they don't have to look far. The streets of the Gaza Strip and the West Bank are teeming with gun-toting militants, sworn to Israel's destruction. For many, the biggest choice may be which militia to join: Hamas or Islamic Jihad. This much seems clear: there will be few alternate futures for these youngsters–and there will be no peace in Israel—until the question of the Palestinians is settled, for once and for all.

ABID KATIB—GETTY IMAGES

SAME OLD, SAME OLD: The sight of a militant in a mask is an everyday reality for these youngsters in the Jabalia refugee camp in the northern Gaza Strip

As a great fundamentalist revival continues to sweep through Islamic cultures, anyone who does not conform to the ethnic and religious mainstream may become outcast. Kurds, above, are scattered among four nations and persecuted to varying degrees in each of them. Their plight may offer a glimpse of the future for all the minorities of the Middle East: Egypt's Copts; Lebanon's Druze and Maronite Christians; and the peaceful, agrarian Marsh Arabs of Iraq, right.

NUPTIALS: Guests in traditional attire enjoy a wedding in Halabja, in the Kurdish region of northern Iraq. The bride, Adnan Baram, 26, and the groom, Arazw Ahmad, 28, lived in Halabja when Saddam Hussein attacked the village with poison gas in 1988; both fled to Iran and survived

GONE FISHIN': Right, Marsh Arab fishermen use floating nets to snare their prey on the al-Hammar marsh, near Basra. The Marsh Arabs are one of the four minorities in Iraq, with Assyrian Christians, Kurds and Sunnis, whose numbers are far outweighed by those of the Shi'ites

Is There Room For Minorities?

Will Iran Always Be Hostile?

فان حزب الله هم الغالبون

MOQAWAMA

المقاومة الإسلامية في لبنان

ST
ISL

D eath to America!" The chant is repeated again and again in today's Iran, a land run by clerics whose ideals are rooted in the 7th century but whose dreams involve nuclear reactors. The election of hard-liner Mahmoud Ahmadinejad to the presidency in 2005 has set his nation on a collision course with Israel and the West. Must the hostility constantly escalate, or can Iran's fanatics—and its reactors—cool down?

Can Iraq Be Stabilized?

Americans remain deeply divided on the subject of their nation's intervention in Iraq, but at least everyone can agree on one point: predictions that U.S. troops would be hailed as liberators and greeted with flowers were exaggerated. In the fall of 2006, as the U.S. mission in Iraq dragged on, no one doubted that the future of this nation held one key to the future of the Middle East. But no one could say what those paired futures might be.

ON DUTY: U.S. soldiers from the 172nd Stryker Brigade, Charlie Company, patrol the streets of Mosul, a perennial hot spot in occupied Iraq

PETER VAN AGTMAEL—POLARIS

Where Are Islam's Women Going?

Seventy years ago, some grandmothers of today's Muslim women fought to remove their veils. Today, as Islam returns to first principles, more and more women of the Middle East are hidden in shrouds—as is their destiny. Will Islam's women ever again seek to emulate their sisters in the West? Or will they continue to remain apart from the world of men?

CLOAKED: Above, since the fall of the Taliban, many women in Afghanistan have shrugged off the full-length burqa, but this woman in conservative Mazar-e-Sharif in the north remains shrouded

EYE OPENER: Right, ophthalmologist Selwa A.F. al-Hazzaa examines a patient in Riyadh, Saudi Arabia. More liberal than her fully veiled assistant, she leaves a portion of her hair uncovered

ASCENDING: At left, graduating Iranian policewomen show off their rappelling skills at the Tehran Police Academy

Will the Walls Ever Come Tumbling Down?

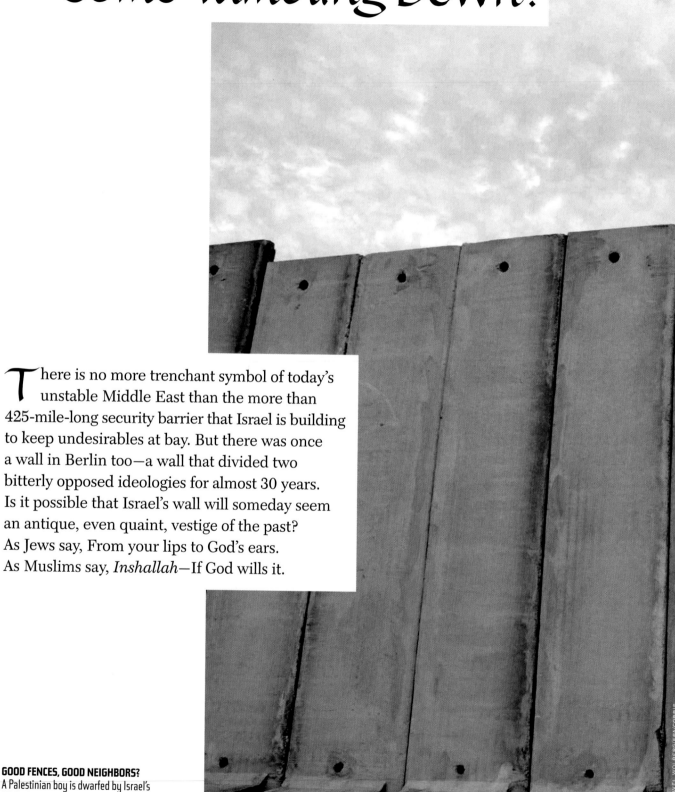

There is no more trenchant symbol of today's unstable Middle East than the more than 425-mile-long security barrier that Israel is building to keep undesirables at bay. But there was once a wall in Berlin too—a wall that divided two bitterly opposed ideologies for almost 30 years. Is it possible that Israel's wall will someday seem an antique, even quaint, vestige of the past? As Jews say, From your lips to God's ears. As Muslims say, *Inshallah*—If God wills it.

GOOD FENCES, GOOD NEIGHBORS?
A Palestinian boy is dwarfed by Israel's 20-ft.-high security barrier near the village of Nazlat Issa

Who Owns the Future?

Jews summon visions of an idyllic tomorrow with the words "Next year in Jerusalem …" Arabs smile at their troubles and say, *"Bukra fil mish-mish"*: Tomorrow there will be apricots. In bad times, both sayings take on the bitter irony of the American phrase "Dream on." But in this region that gave birth to three great religions, visions and dreams—whether of peace or revenge—are more than phantasms. They reverberate in daily life. In a Middle East that is rapidly changing, driven by potent political, economic and religious forces, the final question must be, Which vision of the future will shape the children's dreams? Here's hoping for apricots … in Jerusalem.

ENDANGERED: The Taliban closed girls' schools, like this one in Bamiyan, Afghanistan. As the Taliban regroups, the school is imperiled

TOP GUN: Right, an Iranian boy wearing a Palestinian scarf joins the festivities on "Jerusalem Day," when Iranians celebrate the time to come when Muslims take over Judaism's sacred city

Index

A

Abbas, Mahmoud (Abu Mazen), vi, 39, 43, 115, 117
Abdullah, King, 36, 39, 48, 50
Abdullah II, King, 48
Abraham, 3, 26, 66
Abu Ghraib prison, 113
Aden-Abyan Islamic Army, 60
Aeschylus, 54
Afghanistan, Islamic Emirate of, 58–59
    ethnic groups, 58
    map, 59
    Pakistan and, 58
    poppy harvest (opium), 58–59
    Soviet Union and, 58, 86–87, 97
    Sunni Muslims in, 58
    Taliban, 58–59, 87, 102
    U.S. and, 58–59, 108–9
    women in, 29
Africa
    Muslims in, map, 18–19
    U.S. embassy attacks, 103, 106
Ahmadinejad, Mahmoud, 52, 53, 84, 90, 116, 124
Ahmedzi, Shahpur, 102
Alexander the Great, 53, 58
Ali, Imam, 28
Aliyah, 22
Allah, 22, 27
Allon, Yigal, 41
Americas, Islam in, 18
Amin, Hafizullah, 86–87
Amir, Yigal, 101
al-Anfal campaign, 96
Anglo-Iranian Oil Co., 69
anti-Semitism, 15, 41
al-Aqsa Mosque, 2–3, 74, 104
Arabic language, 25
"Arabization," 96
Arab nationalism, 94
Arab oil embargo, 80–81
Arafat, Yasser, vi, 72–73, 76, 77, 95, 100, 101, 104, 117
    profile, 73
architecture, in the Gulf States, 60
Argov, Shlomo, 92
Asia, Muslims in, map, 18–19
Askariya Mosque, 113
Assad, Bashar, 46–47, 114
Assad, Hafez, 46, 47, 114
Assyrian Christians, 35
Aswan High Dam, 70, 71
Ataturk, Mustafa Kemal, 30, 55, 56, 57, 65
Ayatullah, 22
Azzam, Sheik Abdullah, 97

B

Baath Party, 22, 28, 89
Babylon, 51
Bahrain, Kingdom of, 61
Bakhtiar, Shahpour, 85
Bakr, Abu, 28
al-Bakr, Ahmed Hassan, 50
Balfour, Arthur, 66
Balfour Declaration, 22, 66
Baluchs, 58
Barak, Ehud, 41, 104
Barghouti, Marwan, 117
Bastawisi, Hisham, 38
Bedouins, 22
Begin, Menachem, vi, 41, 67, 90, 100
    Camp David Peace Accords, 82–83
Beirut, Lebanon, 16–17, 44–45
Bellow, Saul, 40

Benedict XVI, Pope, 34, 56
Ben-Gurion, David, 40, 41, 67
Bethlehem, 34
bin Laden, Osama, 6, 30, 64, 87, 91, 102, 108
    Bush, George W., and, 110–11
    Christianity and, 34
    rise to power, 97
    Saudi Arabia and, 36
    Sept. 11 terrorist attacks, 106–7
    U.S. African embassy attacks, 103, 106
    U.S.S. Cole attack, 105, 106
Black September, 30, 48, 76, 77, 94
Blair, Tony, 111
Book of Genesis, 66
Brezhnev, Leonid, 86–97
Britain
    Afghanistan and, 58
    Egypt and, 70–71
    Gulf War and, 98
    Iran and, 69
    Iraq war and, 111
    Libya and, 94
    Ottoman Empire and, 64
    Suez Canal and, 70–71
British Mandate of Palestine, 22
Brzezinski, Zbigniew, 87
Buchenwald death camp, 10–11
Bugti, Nawab Akbar Khan, 58
Burckhardt, Johann Ludwig, 49
Burj al-Arab (Arabian Tower), 60–61
burqas, 22
Bush, George H.W., 89
    Gulf War and, 55, 98–99
Bush, George W., 33, 105, 116, 117
    bin Laden and, 106, 110–11
    Egypt and, 38, 39
    Iraq and, 51, 112–13
    Iraq war and, 110–11
    Palestinians and, 115
    Taliban and, 108–9
Byzantine Empire, 57

C

Caliph, 22, 28
Camp David Accords (1978), vi, 38, 40, 82–83
Cana (Lebanon), 45
Canada, oil reserves, 33
Carter, Howard, 39
Carter, Jimmy, vi–1, 82–83, 85, 87
Carter Doctrine, 32
Casey, George, 113
Cedar Revolution, 45, 114
Chamoun, Camille, 45
Christianity, 34–35
    Crusades and, 6
    Islam and, 26, 34–35
    minority religions, 35
Church of the Holy Sepulchre, 2–3, 34–35
CIA, in Iran, 69
Clinton, Bill, 100, 103, 104, 106
Constantinople, 57
Cooperative Council for Arab States of the Gulf, 60
Coptic Christians, 35, 38, 124
Crusades, 6–7, 34
Cyrus the Great, 53

D

Dahab, Egypt, terrorist attacks, 38
Damascus, 34
Darius I, 53
Dayan, Moshe, 79, 101, 115

profile, 75
Diaspora, 11, 66, 121
Dome of the Rock, 22
Druze, 44, 124
Dubai, 60–61

E

Eden, Anthony, 71
Egypt, ancient, tombs, 39
Egypt, Arab Republic of, 38–39
    Britain and, 70–71
    Camp David Accords and, 82–83
    Coptic Christians, 35, 38
    Dahab terrorist attacks, 38
    domestic terrorism, 38–39
    France and, 70–71
    Israel and, 38, 39, 70–71, 74–75, 78–79
    map, 39
    militant Islamism in, 91
    Six-Day War, 74–75
    Soviet Union and, 70, 71
    Suez Canal, 70–71
    tourism, 38, 39
    U.S. and, vi–1, 38, 39
Eisenhower, Dwight D., 44, 45, 69, 71
emir, 22
Erdogan, Recep Tayyip, 56, 57
Eshkol, Levi, 40, 41, 74
European Union
    Palestine and, 43
    Turkey and, 56, 57

F

Faisal, King, 50, 64
    profile, 81
Falastin (Palestine), 42
Farouk, King, 70
Fatah (Movement for the Liberation of Palestine), 22, 73, 76, 100, 117
fatwa, 22
fedayeen, 70
Federally Administered Tribal Areas, Pakistan, 58
First Caliph, 28
FitzGerald, Peter, 114
Five Pillars of Islam, 27
France
    Egypt and, 70–71
    Ottoman Empire and, 64
    paratroopers bombed in Lebanon, 93
    Suez Canal and, 70–71
Franks, Tommy, 111

G

Gaddafi, Muammar, 94
Garden of Eden, 51
Gaza Strip, 43, 100
    Israel-Hizballah conflict over, 119
    Israel's withdrawal from, 40, 115
    Palestinians and, 41
Genghis Khan, 58
Germany, 10–11
Giuliani, Rudolph, 106
Golan Heights, 74, 75
Gorbachev, Mikhail, 87
Greater Israel, 101
Green Zone, Iraq, 51
Gulf States, 60–61
    map, 61
Gulf War, 1991
    Kurds and, 55
    Operation Desert Shield, 98

Operation Desert Storm, 98–99
Saudi Arabia and, 36

H

Hadith, 22, 26
Haganah, 66
Haidar, Rustem, 64
hajj (pilgrimage to Mecca), 5, 22, 27, 36
Halaby, Lisa (Queen Noor), 49
Halaby, Najeeb, 49
Hamas, 22, 31, 43, 100, 115
    election of (2006), 117
    Mubarak and, 39
ul-Haq, Mohammed Zia, 87
Harakat al Tahrir al-Falastin, 72–73
Haram al-Sharif, 104
Har Homa, Israel, 121
Hariri, Rafik, 44–45, 46, 114
Hawass, Zawi, 39
Hegira (journey to Mecca), 27
Herzl, Theodor, 41
Hirshfeld, Yair, 100
Hizballah, 16, 22, 31
    Iran and, 52
    Israel and, 40, 41, 118–19
    in Lebanon, 44–45, 93, 114–15
    Mubarak's views on, 39
    murder of U.S. Marines by, 44, 45
    Syria and, 46
Holocaust, 10–11
"honor killings," 29
Hubbert, King, 32
Hubbert's Peak, 32
Hussein, King, 48, 49, 72, 75, 76, 79

I

Ibn Saud, King, 36, 37
Idris, King, 94
imam, 22
intifadeh, 22, 95, 101, 104
Iran, Islamic Republic of, 52–53
    economy, 52
    elections (2005), 116
    Hizballah and, 52
    Iran-Iraq war, 88–89, 98
    map, 53
    Muslim fundamentalists, 53
    nationalization of oil, 69
    nuclear capability, 1, 53, 90
    oil reserves, 33
    revolution, 85
    Shi'ite Muslims, 52–53
    Sunni Muslims, 53
    Syria and, 46
    U.S. and, 68–69, 84–85, 116
    U.S. hostage crisis, 84–85
    women, 29, 126
Iran, Shah of. See Pahlavi, Mohammed Reza (Shah of Iran)
Iran-contra scheme, 89
Iran-Iraq war, 85, 88–89, 98
Iraq, Republic of, 8
    background, 50–51
    boundary designations, 64
    civil war, 51
    claim to Kuwait, 50
    creation of, 50
    Gulf War, 1991, 98–99
    insurgency, 112–13
    Iran-Iraq war, 88–89, 98
    Israel and, 50, 74–75, 90
    Kurds, 50, 55, 96
    map, 51